THE FIRST BUDDHIST WOMEN

THE FIRST BUDDHIST WOMEN
Translations and Commentaries
on the *Therigatha*

SUSAN MURCOTT

Parallax Press
Berkeley, California

Printed in the United States of America

Parallax Press
P.O. Box 7355
Berkeley, CA 94707

Cover Design by Gay Reineck
Book Design by Ayelet Maida
Map on page xii by Gay Reineck

LIBRARY OF CONGRESS CATALOGING-IN-PUBLICATION DATA
Tipitaka. Suttapitaka. Khuddakanikaya. Therigatha. English.
    The First Buddhist Women : translations and
commentaries on the Therigatha / by Susan Murcott.
        p.   cm.
    Translation of: Therigatha.
    Includes bibliogaphical references and index.
    ISBN 0-938077-42-2 : $14.00
    1. Tipitaka. Suttapitaka Khuddakanikaya. Therigatha—
Commentaries. I. Murcott, Susan. II. Title.
BQ1452.E5M87   1991
294.3'823--dc20   91-10819
                                                        CIP

5   6   7   8   9   10   /   01   00   99   98

Dedicated to my mother and father,
who encouraged and supported me
in exploring the wide world freely.

Preface

This book grew out of my need to find a meaningful philosophical and religious belief system. It took ten years to bring together in terms of the inner work, and five years to write. I grew up in an American middle-class home of love and luxury, and I was raised on a church-on-Sundays Protestantism. But I came of age in the '60s, in the shadow of the assassinations of the two Kennedys and Martin Luther King, Jr., and of the Vietnam War. I think it was this contrast between my "good life" and the terrible suffering in the world that led me to identify with the Buddha-legend of the wealthy prince who was blind to suffering until he encountered an old man, a sick man, a corpse, and finally a renunciant.

My own small efforts to stop the Vietnam War led to a number of important friends and influences, including Louise Forrest, Anne Narduli, and Katie Stokely. These three Boston housemates, all struggling with the issue of women and ministry, directly influenced this book. Louise had been an Episcopal nun and was associated with some of the first, controversially-ordained Episcopal women priests. In this same period in Boston, Sister Marie Augusta Neal, a spokeswoman for Catholic radicals, was posing brilliant challenges to theological and papal arguments that women should be excluded from episcopal and priestly office because Jesus was a man, because his twelve disciples were men, because Mary was not at the Last Supper, and for other sexist reasons. Mary Daly, Rosemary Reuther, and other Christian feminist theologians were speaking publicly and taught or frequently spoke in Boston.

While I admired the spirit of my Christian feminist friends, I found the barriers of Christian tradition, dogma, and belief insurmountable. I sought a system of faith that would contain at least these two elements: (1) an affirmation that women could understand and attain the highest religious truths, and (2) institutional structures that gave women equal opportunity to manifest spiritual authority in any and all religious roles and offices. My own tradition of Christianity was not providing either of these essential supports for women's spirituality.

My search led me to Buddhism, not as an endpoint, but as an important and shaping discovery. In 1977, I stumbled upon the first English translation of the *Therigatha* in the Library at the University of Melbourne. Caroline Rhys Davids' translation had been published in London in 1909. The other complete version in English of this text was a scholarly translation by K.R. Norman, published in 1971. Unsatisfied with the inaccessibility of the language in both translations, I decided to rework a few of the verses myself. Although this began as a small editing project, it quickly led to the study of Pali, the primary language in which the Buddhist scriptures have been preserved. The present book began to take shape around this project.

The *Therigatha* is the enlightenment poetry of the Buddhist nuns of the sixth century B.C.E. To my knowledge, it is the earliest known collection of women's religious poetry. This book is an effort of translation, not only in the common sense of the word—the turning from one language into another—but in the primary meaning of translation—a transference. THE FIRST BUDDHIST WOMEN is an attempt to transfer and communicate to Western readers a religious text that has had profound meaning in various Asian cultures over a span of 2,500 years. To me, the *Therigatha* is a treasure because it is something I sought and could not find in my own culture. This book, a labor of love, is a record of my discovery.

ACKNOWLEDGMENTS

THE FIRST BUDDHIST WOMEN could not have been realized without the continuous help, support, guidance, and enthusiasm of friends. Especially it could not have taken form without the help of two people: Roger Milliken Jr. and John Tarrant. Roger gave his time generously to work through the Pali text of the *Therigatha* word by word, thereby teaching me the rudiments of Pali. I will always be indebted to him for his kindness. John, a talented poet with a gift for making words on a page come alive, helped me rework each translation after I grasped the meaning in the original. It was through their help over a two-year period that the poems that form the core of this book were translated.

In addition, I would like to acknowledge the kind help of the following people;

Judy Hurley, who first taught me about Buddhism;

Meredith McKinney and Deborah Hopkinson, who supported this work before any of us really knew where it would lead, and served as gentle critics as the book took shape;

Phra Khantipalo and Ayya Khema, who introduced me to Theravada Buddhism and the *Pali Canon;*

Robert Aitken, my teacher and dear friend, who himself is engaged in the translation of Japanese Zen culture to the West;

Anne Aitken, and the members of the Diamond Sangha;

Cornelia Dimmitt of Georgetown University and the monks of Wat Pah Nanachat, who offered extensive comments and editorial assistance;

China Galland, who encouraged me to bring the completed manuscript down from the attic and then sent it off herself to Arnie Kotler at Parallax Press.

Finally, I thank my husband and companion in life, Ralph Coffman, whose love and unfailing support of the work allowed it to come to fruition.

S. M.
Marblehead, Massachusetts
January 1991

Contents

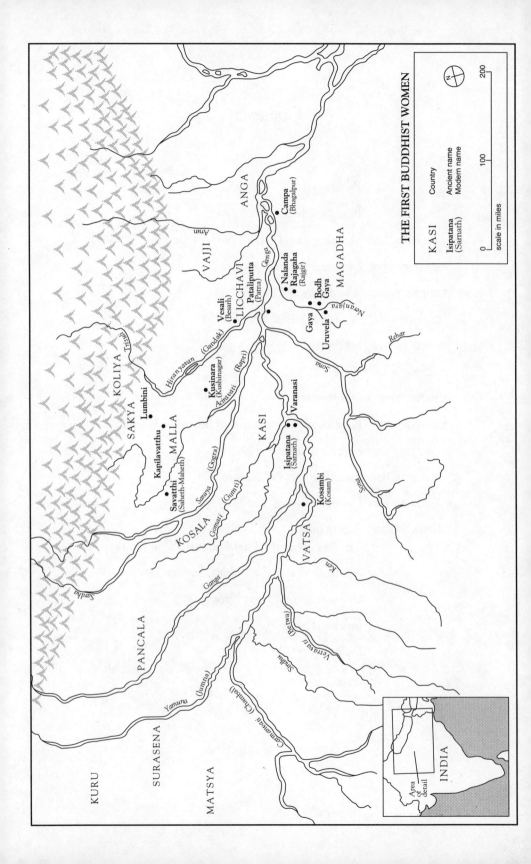

THE FIRST BUDDHIST WOMEN

KASI   Country

Isipatana   Ancient name
(Sarnath)   Modern name

scale in miles
0   100   200

THE FIRST BUDDHIST WOMEN

Introduction

THE FIRST BUDDHIST WOMEN is a study of the *Therigatha*, a collection of seventy-three poems in the canon of the earliest Buddhist literature. *Theri* means "women elders," or "women who have grown old in knowledge," and *gatha* means "verse," "stanza," or "song." Hence the *Therigatha* are the poems of the wise women of early Buddhism. In force and beauty, these religious poems rank with the best of Indian lyric poetry, from the hymns of the *Rigveda* to the lyrical poems of Kalidasa and Amaru.

The *Therigatha* was passed on orally for six centuries before being committed to writing in Sri Lanka in the first century B.C.E. in the literary language of Pali. The entire collection of the Pali Buddhist Canon is called the *Tipitaka* (lit. "the three baskets").[1]

Like all Buddhist scriptures, the *Therigatha* finds its source in the life of Siddhartha Gautama, the historical Buddha. There are no records of when he was born, but Theravadin, or Southern Buddhists, reckon that he lived from 560-480 B.C.E., while Mahayana, or Northern Buddhists, maintain that his dates were 460-380 B.C.E. Both traditions agree that he lived for eighty years.

Siddhartha Gautama was born not into a king's, but into a Sakyan chief's family in Kapilavatthu. Tradition has it that at sixteen, he married a woman his same age, Yasodhara, the daughter of a nobleman's family. By her, Siddhartha gave birth to one son, Rahula. At age twenty-nine, on the outskirts of his family home, Siddhartha saw first an old man, next a sick man, then a corpse. Following these sights of suffering, he saw an ascetic. Soon thereafter, because his heart was not at peace regarding the great questions of birth, suffering, old age, and death, Siddhartha left his home, wife, and child, following a tradition that was ancient in India even at that time, that of the *samana*, the renunciant. Six years later, after studying with the leading renunciants of his day and feeling unsatisfied with their teaching, Siddhartha resolved to sit alone under a bodhi tree until he either died or realized the highest truth. It was under that tree that he attained *nirvana*, the extinction of greed, hatred, and ignorance. From this point on he was a *buddha*, one who has attained complete enlightenment.[2]

3

There are two kinds of buddhas: *paccekabuddhas*, who have attained complete enlightenment but who do not teach in the world, and *sammasambuddhas*, who are also completely enlightened but dedicate themselves to proclaiming the saving truth to all beings. Gautama would be considered a *sammasambuddha* because, following his enlightenment, he decided not to renounce the world completely, but to teach to others what he had discovered for himself. He chose to be a *sattharo*, a "teacher." According to Buddhist tradition, such teachers appear on Earth from time to time. Their purpose is to teach *dharma*, the "law" or "doctrine" which is the truth, the only Reality.

Like other *sammasambuddhas*, Gautama founded a *sangha*, a community of monks (*bhikkhus*) and nuns (*bhikkhunis*), laymen and laywomen.

Gautama preached his first sermon to five fellow renunciants, men who had been his fellow practitioners before he set out on his own path. Convinced by his teaching, they were ordained by him and became his first disciples. Laywomen and laymen were the next category of followers. Because ordination of women was not permitted at first, nuns were the last group to come into the fold. The full story of the formation of the Order of Nuns introduces Chapter One.

The nuns' sangha was a radical experiment for its time. In its earliest phase, it consisted of *samani*, "female wanderers" who could live in the forest alone.[3] Women like Bhadda Kundalakesa, Nanduttara, Dantika, Uppalavanna, and Sukka did so. (Later, rules prohibiting nuns' independent wandering were formulated.)[4] However, it was more usual for nuns (and, for that matter, monks) to form into communities in or on the outskirts of villages.

The nuns patterned their community after the monks' community. Like monks, nuns were allowed three saffron robes, a belt and razor, a bowl, thread and needle, and a water filter. In addition, nuns were allowed the use of a hip-string during menstruation. Like the monks, nuns lived in cells, sometimes individual cells, sometimes with a *saddhiviharini*, a co-resident or roommate. Their dwellings were humble shacks of mud and reeds. They lived near villages, where they would go on daily almsround to be offered cooked rice, barley, wheat, beans, rye, fruits, or vegetables. Nuns could not accept ghee, oil, honey, fish, meat, milk, or curds unless they were ill.

The term *bhikkhuni sangha* can mean all Buddhist nuns everywhere or the nuns of a particular locale. There were many communities in different locations, each with at least five nuns living within the same boundary, district, or locale. A *parivenavasika* or *gana* was a group of two, three, or four nuns. This did not constitute a "complete" order and therefore could not confer ordination.

THE TEXT

The *Therigatha* was composed and preserved according to a strict form. The *gathas* ("songs") were descriptive rather than lyrical or presentational, and could sometimes be very technical. The songs were not spoken, but chanted. However, some lines originally may have been sayings (roughly comparable to the *Sayings* tradition of Jesus) that were converted from prose to metric form to facilitate recollection. In other words, although gathas do represent the earliest stratum of the *Pali Canon*, gathas may not have been the form of the original utterances.

The verses of the *Therigatha* today are the ones that survived six centuries of oral transmission. Their exact history and how they came into their present form can only be guessed. We are confronted with utterances that were considered worth repeating and therefore memorized and passed down. Incorporated into original material were many "stock phrases," verses that belonged to a common pool of religious literature of the day.[5]

Each stanza (*sloka*) of the *Therigatha* consists of four verses (*padas*) of eight syllables each. The first and second *padas* form one line, divided by a caesura, followed by the second line, which consists of the third and fourth *padas*. Here is an example:

> *sukham supahi therike | katva colena paruta |*
> *upasanto hi te rago | sukkhadakam va kumbhiyam ||*

INDIAN BUDDHIST HISTORY

Indian Buddhism can be divided into three distinct periods. The phases of early or primitive Buddhism extends from the Buddha's enlightenment and first conversions (ca. late sixth century B.C.E.) to the era of the great Emperor Asoka's patronage of Buddhism (ca.

272-236 B.C.E.). During this stage, the teachings of the Buddha and his renowned followers were collected, arranged, elaborated, and committed to memory. This oral tradition was meticulously maintained and passed down by certain individuals, female as well as male, particularly gifted in the recall of what would have constituted whole volumes of written material.

During the second period of Indian Buddhism (ca. third century B.C.E. to third century C.E.), in about 80 B.C.E.,[6] these scriptures were committed to writing. Though the common tongue of Siddhartha Gautama and his earliest followers, who were all from the middle Ganges region, was Magadhi, the Buddhist scriptures were first recorded in the literary language of Pali, which, though it shows traces of Magadhi, is a different language. Pali (lit. "holy scripture") is a form of the ancient Paishachi tongue then common in Western India. Sermons that had been delivered by the Buddha in Magadhi were, during the first centuries after his death, translated by Western Indian converts into Paishachi, which in turn developed into Pali.

During the third phase of Indian Buddhism (third century C.E. to tenth century C.E.), adaptations, interpretations, and commentaries on the original teaching and practices flourished, then waned. In the fifth century, Dhammapala, of Kancipuram, wrote a commentary in Pali on the *Therigatha*, as part of his larger work, the *Paramatthandipani*, or "Elucidation of the Ultimate Meaning." In it, he prefixed each poem of the women elders with a narrative story. The story included a sketch of that particular woman's life and the circumstances that led her to become a Buddhist sister. Dhammapala tells us that he drew his material from three older commentaries. The true source was the oral tradition, the body of inherited folklore that consisted of legends of antiquity probably based on a kernel of historical fact. Around the names and poems of the nuns of the *Therigatha*, there has been a cumulative growth of myth and legend. Some of the nuns' stories were also recorded elsewhere in the *Pali Canon*, as well as in the *Manoratha Purani*. On the whole, Dhammapala's work is considered by modern *Therigatha* scholars to be quite accurate.[7]

PALI BUDDHIST STUDIES IN THE WEST

"During the first fifteen hundred years of its history, Buddhism, perhaps the most powerful movement of ideas in the history of Asia, neither drew specific attack from the civilized West nor contributed positively to the formation of European thought system," according to Guy Welbon in *The Buddhist Nirvana and Its Western Interpreters*.[8] In fact, there was no appreciable European study of Buddhism until the nineteenth century, when Thomas W. Rhys Davids, an English civil servant in Sri Lanka from 1864 to 1877, collected a complete version of the Pali *Tipitaka* as existed in palm-leaf manuscripts. When he returned to England in 1881, he founded the Pali Text Society, to foster the cooperation of scholars in the transliteration of Pali into Roman letters and the translation and publication of Pali Buddhist texts in English. It was through his initial efforts, and later the efforts of his wife, Caroline, who succeeded him as president of the Pali Text Society, that, during the course of six decades, the nearly complete transliteration, translation, and publication of the Pali texts occurred.

The palm-leaf manuscripts of the *Therigatha* were transliterated with scholarly care in 1883, by Professor R. Pischel of Berlin. Working with his edition plus the one (incomplete) copy of Dhammapala's commentary extant in Europe at that time, then later from a complete copy purchased in Burma, Caroline Rhys Davids undertook the first translation of the *Therigatha* into English. After she completed it, a noted publisher declined even to read the manuscript. Deciding that this boded ill for support from other publishing firms, they decided to inaugurate a series and publish it themselves.

Caroline Rhys Davids' translation of the *Therigatha* was published in 1909. Highly commendable for a first effort, it is literally accurate while being sensitive to poetic expression, although now the English is quite dated.

A second complete translation of the *Therigatha* into English was accomplished in 1971 by K.R. Norman, also as a part of the Pali Text Society's translation series. It is a critical edition, in which the author has "produced a literal, almost word-for-word translation."[9] Some of the poems have also been translated by Phra Khantipalo, Barbara Stoler Miller, and others. The present translation is intended to complement the work of Caroline Rhys Davids and K.R.

Norman, while presenting the poetry in contemporary English easily accessible to a general rather than scholarly audience.

Before turning to the poems themselves, there remain several outstanding questions about the ascription of each particular poem in the *Therigatha* to a particular nun. First—did the particular nun whose name appears at the end of each poem (in the original text) create that poem? To understand this issue, we must recognize that we are dealing with an ancient and non-Western culture. The Buddhist devotee was not interested in her or his individuality, but rather in attaining the Buddha's experience. Indians did not have the concept of ownership of particular words or poems. There were, of course, no copyrights, and anyone could repeat a poem or borrow lines from someone else's utterances. Thus the ascription of a certain poem to a certain author in the *Therigatha* does not guarantee that person actually composed the poem. Tradition asserts that the person uttered the poem, nothing more.

A second question is—are the nuns of the *Therigatha* historical or legendary figures? Of the seventy-two nuns to whom poems are attributed in the *Therigatha*, there are only twenty in other works of the *Pali Canon*. *Therigatha* poems are repeated in the *Apadana*, a canonical text of forty life histories of the sisters, though the names do not correspond in seventeen! Nor again do name and poem agree in the versions of the sisters' poems in the *Samyutta*. While some of the sisters are indeed elusive historically, there is no need to doubt the existence of a considerable number of them. Some of the poems of the *Therigatha* refer to the author in the poem itself, either by naming her or by making a pun on her name. K.R.Norman cites thirty-two poems which appear to acknowledge the author in this way.[10]

A third question of ascription is that raised by K.E.Neumann[11] and K.R. Norman,[12] as to whether these poems were really composed by women at all. While the Buddhist tradition is indisputably male-dominated, this is, nonetheless, a sexist concern. The same scholars never ask, for example, whether the *Theragatha* was uttered by women. Two other Pali scholars offer their opinions:

> Not often since the patriarchal age set in has woman succeeded in so breaking through her barriers as to set on lasting record the expression of herself and of things as they appeared

to her. But to assume that, because this happened seldom, therefore, this collection of documents, though ascribed to her, are necessarily not by her, is to carry over far the truth.[13]

There can be no doubt that the great majority of the 'Songs of the Lady Elders' were composed by women. First of all, the monks never had so much sympathy with the female members of the community, as to warrant our crediting them with having composed these songs sung from the very hearts of women. We need only recall the difficulties which, according to tradition, Gautama placed in the way of his foster-mother when she desired to found the order of nuns, and the reproaches which were cast at Ananda in several parts of the Canon on account of his friendly attitude towards women. For the same reason it would never have occurred to the monks to ascribe songs to the women, if an incontestible tradition had not pointed at this direction.[14]

STRUCTURE AND PURPOSE OF THE BOOK

THE FIRST BUDDHIST WOMEN includes sixty-one of the seventy-three poems from the *Therigatha*. There were several criteria for the inclusion of sixty-one and the exclusion of twelve. The first was literary; I chose the translations that made good poems in English. Several *gathas* seemed tedious or mechanical—sometimes in the original, sometimes in the translation—and these were not included. In addition, where two poems seemed almost identical (e.g. the poems of Mitta and Bhadra, Uttara and the Thirty Nuns under Patacara), or where a poem was a composite of stock verses already encountered in one or several other poems (e.g. Another Sama, Another Uttama, and a few others), these also were not included. Finally the two final and very long poems of the *Therigatha* collection, those attributed to Isidasi and Sumedha, were not included because they generally are held to be later poems, perhaps composed in the third century B.C.E.

This book contains the histories or legends of the nuns themselves. The primary source for these stories was Caroline Rhys Davids' translation of Dhammapala's *Therigatha Commentary*. Bits and pieces of the women's stories were also gleaned from the *Pali Dictionary of Proper Names* and from other sources in the *Pali Canon*. Indeed, with the exception of the *Sutta Nipata*, nuns are mentioned in every canonical work!

After completing the translations of the poems and selecting the stories to accompany them, it was difficult to decide in what form to present the material. The Pali Text Society's two English translations follow the organizational method of the *Therigatha* itself, where the verses are grouped according to the number of stanzas per poem. Although this may have served well as an mnemonic aid in the oral tradition, on the printed page it seems a boring and arbitrary way to encounter poetry. Therefore, this volume diverges from tradition, and arranges the poems and stories into chapters based on the roles and relationships of the women.

This book is a record, for Western readers, of a major religious tradition in women's spirituality, based on the equality of women and men in the realm of the spirit and women's ability to assume spiritual authority in the secular context.

The model that the nuns of the *Therigatha* provide is one where women have the capacity to realize and understand the highest religious goals of their faith in the same roles and to the same degrees as men. In Buddhism, women can form celibate communities, teach, be ordained and ordain, preach, gather disciples, and create religious poetry of great force. Isolated examples of powerful religious women can be discovered in our own Western Judeo-Christian traditions as well, but the *Therigatha* is unique as a collection of original material documenting these achievements at the source of one of the world's great religious traditions. While the religion's founder was a man, the nuns of the *Therigatha* were his friends, relatives, and contemporaries. And, insofar as they uttered *buddhavacana*, "the words of an enlightened one," they were his spiritual equals. THE FIRST BUDDHIST WOMEN, then, is an effort to share with contemporary readers how one world religion acknowledged from its very beginning the authority and equality of women in spiritual practice.

---

[1] The *Tipitaka* consists of three large sections: (1) the *vinaya-pitaka*, or basket of the rules of the monastic order, (2) the *sutta-pitaka*, or basket of sayings, sermons, or essential teachings of the Buddha and his eminent followers, and (3) the *abhidharma-pitaka*, or basket of philosophical treatises and commentaries. The *sutta-pitaka* itself consists of five collections, and the *Therigatha*, along with the *Theragatha*, a similar though larger compilation of verses of monks, falls within the last of these. Strictly speaking, a *sutta* is a short prose saying, but here and there, the *sutta-pitaka* is interrupted by *gathas*,

poems understood to be the most ancient layer of Buddhist teaching. Hence the *Therigatha* is an excellent window into original Buddhism, and the chief source for the study of the first Buddhist women.

2 The term "buddha" occurs only once in reference to Siddhartha Gautama in the earliest strata of the *Pali Canon*, the *Atthakavagga* and *Parayanavagga*. In the *Atthakavagga*, Siddhartha is called Gautama, or "Bhagava," meaning "Blessed One" or "Lord." The word "buddha" is used to describe anyone who has attained enlightenment. The term is appellative, not a proper name. But the word "buddha" soon became specifically applied to Gautama.

In THE FIRST BUDDHIST WOMEN, following the usage of the earlier texts, we will refer to Siddhartha Gautama either as Gautama, to underscore the fact that he was a human being, or, following the tradition, we will call him "the Buddha." The capitalization of "b" in the name is a phenomenon of translation into English.

3 Even in the earliest days of Buddhism, the ideal of the homeless wanderer was not one of escape from the world. The *Atthakavvagga*, a very early text, speaks of the *samana/samani* or *muni*, sage, not as a hermit who goes to the forest to escape from the world, but as the vigilant person who lives in the world without submitting to its myriad temptations.

4 See Appendix for "Rules of the Nuns' Sangha."

5 According to I.B. Horner, "It is now generally agreed that since the same line or lines occur now and again in other verses widely distributed throughout the *Pali Canon*, there must have been a time, probably before writing came into vogue, when a common stock of floating funds of verses was in existence. From these the poet or compiler of poems ...could draw at his or her pleasure....Such repetitions, which are in no sense piratical, among so much that is individual, are to be accepted as an interesting part of the literary heritage handed down in the *Pali Canon*." Horner, I.B. *Early Buddhist Poetry*. (Sri Lanka: Ananda Semage, 1963), p. 3.

6 Rhys Davids, Caroline. *Psalms of the Sisters*. (London: Henry Frowde, Oxford University Press Warehouse, 1909), p. xvi.

7 Burlingame, Eugene. *Buddhaghosa's Dhammapada Commentary (Dhammapadatthakatha)*. (3 volumes). Harvard Oriental Series, Volume 28. (Cambridge: Harvard University Press, 1921), p. 56.

8 Welbon, Guy. *The Buddhist Nirvana and Its Western Interpreters*. (Chicago: University of Chicago Press, 1968).

9 Norman, K.R. *The Elder's Verses II*. (London: Luzak and Company, Ltd., 1971), p. xxxix.

10 *Ibid.*, p. xxi-xxii.

11 Neumann, K.E. *Die Lieder der Monche und Nonnen Gotamo Buddho's*. (Berlin, 1899).

12 Norman, K.R. *Op. Cit.*, p. xix.

[13] Caroline Rhys Davids. *Op. Cit.*, p. xxiii.

[14] Winternitz, Maurice. *History of Indian Literature*. (New Delhi: V.K. Batra, 1972), p. 100.

CHAPTER ONE

Mahapajapati Gotami & Her Disciples

Mahapajapati Gotami, who was to become the founder of the first order of Buddhist nuns, was born into the Koliyan clan in the town of Devadaha in northeastern India near the foothills of the Himalayas. At her birth, an astrologer foretold that she would be the leader of a large following, and she was named Pajapati, meaning "leader of a great assembly." "Maha," a prefix which means "great," came to be used with her name. It was further prophesied of her, as it had been of her older sister Maya, that she would be the mother of a great secular or religious ruler.

Pajapati and her sister, Maya, grew up, were both married to a chief of the Sakyan clan, Suddhodana, and lived with him in the capital town of Kapilavatthu. According to Buddhist legend, Suddhodana was a great king, and his son, Siddhartha, was his prince and heir. In fact, in the Sakyan clan, any male was eligible to be chief—it was a position elected by rotation. The only true king of that region was Pasenadi, King of Kosala, who was overlord of the states which included the Sakyan and Koliyan clans. Maya's and Pajapati's marriage was into a clan similar to their own. Both clans were small and did not observe caste distinctions. Clan members worked at agriculture, wielded arms when necessary, and traded in nearby provinces.

Maya was the first to become pregnant. As was customary, Maya wanted to give birth in her family home, so when her time was near, she undertook the journey to Devadaha. En route, she stopped in the Lumbini Garden to rest and admire the flowering trees. When she raised her arm to pick a blossoming branch of an asoka tree, she felt her initial labor pains and gave birth to a boy under the tree. (Over two centuries later, the Buddhist Emperor Asoka set up a pillar to mark that site. Since the pillar survives today, it is possible to identify the place exactly.)

When they heard the news back in Kapilavatthu, Suddhodana and everyone else were overjoyed at the birth of a son. The chief immediately called a famous seer, Asita, who declared that if the child remained at home, he would become a secular ruler; if he left home, he would become a great religious teacher, the Buddha. The newborn was named Siddhartha, which means "he who accomplishes his aim."

But seven days after her delivery, Maya died. Neither history nor legend tells us why. Pajapati took Siddhartha and raised him as her own first child, and later bore two more children, a daughter named Sundari-Nanda and a son named Nanda.

Many years passed. At the age of twenty-nine, Siddhartha left home and did not return during the six years of his religious quest. His foster-mother was in her fifties or early sixties when Siddhartha finally came back to Kapilavatthu. Upon his return, he was treated cooly. His wife, Yasodhara, did not embrace him but sent their son, Rahula, to meet him. The Sakyan clan, known for its pride and religious conservatism, was skeptical of the novel teachings of a once favorite son. Pajapati no doubt would have been sensitive to all the varying reactions. Her own response was to welcome him. Suddhodana did also, and when the Buddha preached to them, both were moved by his teachings and became converts.

By this time, Pajapati would not only have been eminent as the wife of the chieftain, but would also have been respected for her age. After she became a lay convert to her son's new teachings, she may have been held in even greater esteem as a woman who had rare access to religious instruction and practice.

One by one or in groups, women sought Pajapati's support, advice, and direction. These women appealed to her not merely because of her high status. She shared with them—and after her husband died, she may have exemplified for them—the particular anxiety of being a woman without any primary male relations. Following the Buddha's return to Kapilavatthu, Pajapati's son, Nanda, and her grandnephew, Rahula, had both become monks. Not long after this, Suddhodana died. This left Pajapati without the web of family connections that gave every woman in that society her identity and security. We find this supposition confirmed when we review the poems of this chapter. The majority of the authors are women formerly of Siddhartha Gautama's harem, women who lost their sense of identity when their primary patron set out on his spiritual journey.

Next, a significant event occurred which brought even more women to Pajapati's door. An angry dispute had arisen between the

Sakyans and their neighboring Koliyans over the right to draw water from the major river of that region. A battle ensued in which
men were killed. Some women who lost their husbands came to
Pajapati. Others went to the Buddha and urged him to try to settle
the dispute. The Buddha, related not only to the Sakyans but also,
through Maya and Pajapati, to the Koliyans, delivered an inspiring
sermon. As a result, many of the men renounced fighting altogether
and became Buddhist monks. But this left yet another group of
Sakyan and Koliyan women without husbands or other primary male
relations.

Altogether, the number of women who had come to Pajapati by
this time totaled "five hundred," a number frequently used to mean
a great many. No doubt some came simply for comfort and support,
others came to resolve ultimate questions of birth, suffering, and
death, yet others sought a new family with women they trusted and
with whom they shared common experience. The longing of these
women, whatever form it took, became their spiritual aspiration. All
would have had a personal story, most of which are now lost, and a
particular experience of what the Buddha called the "First Noble
Truth." This is what motivated them to join with Pajapati in the
new and radical way she was about to suggest.

Pajapati recognized the powerful conjunction of events and
people. An old but influential woman without further worldly obligations, she was surrounded by displaced wives, widows, consorts,
dancers, and musicians. Lacking other kin, these women were turning to her and to one another. Having fully grasped this situation,
Pajapati decided to take the following course, recounted in the
Cullavagga:

> Now at one time the Buddha was staying among the Sakyans
> at Kapilavatthu in the Banyan Monastery. Mahapajapati
> Gotami went to the place where the Buddha was, approached
> and greeted him, and, standing at a respectful distance, spoke
> to him: "It would be good, Lord, if women could be allowed to
> renounce their homes and enter into the homeless state under
> the Dharma and discipline of the Tathagata." [Note: see
> *pabbajati* in Glossary.]
>
> "Enough, Gotami. Don't set your heart on women being
> allowed to do this."

[A second and a third time Pajapati made the same request in the same words and received the same reply.] And thinking that the Blessed One would not allow women to enter into homelessness, she bowed to him, and keeping her right side towards him, departed in tears.

Then the Blessed One set out for Vesali. Pajapati cut off her hair, put on saffron-colored robes, and headed for Vesali with a number of Sakyan women. She arrived at Kutagara Hall in the Great Grove with swollen feet and covered with dust. Weeping, she stood there outside the Hall.

Seeing her standing there, the venerable Ananda asked, "Why are you crying?"

"Because, Ananda, the Blessed One does not permit women to renounce their homes and enter into the homeless state under the Dharma and discipline proclaimed by the Tathagata."

Then the Venerable Ananda went to the Buddha, bowed before him, and took his seat to one side. He said, "Pajapati is standing outside under the entrance porch with swollen feet, covered with dust, and crying because you do not permit women to renounce their homes and enter into the homeless state. It would be good, Lord, if women were to have permission to do this."

"Enough, Ananda. Don't set your heart on women being allowed to do this."

[A second and a third time Ananda made the same request in the same words and received the same reply.]

Then Ananda thought: The Blessed one does not give his permission. Let me try asking on other grounds.

"Are women able, Lord, when they have entered into homelessness to realize the fruits of stream-entry, once-returning, non-returning, and arahantship?"

"Yes, Ananda, they are able."

"If women then are able to realize perfection, and since Pajapati was of great service to you—she was your aunt, nurse, foster mother; when your mother died, she even suckled you at her own breast—it would be good if women could be allowed to enter into homelessness."

"If then, Ananda, Pajapati accepts the Eight Special Rules,[1] let that be reckoned as her ordination."[2]

It must have been evident to the Buddha that Pajapati and the group of women with her, who had walked one hundred fifty miles barefoot, with heads shaved and the saffron-colored robes of the already ordained, would not accept "no" for an answer. The sight of these women and their unshakable sincerity must have made a vivid impression, and not only on the sympathetic Ananda. Their resolve was audacious in a culture where humility and obedience were desirable traits in women. Perhaps the Eight Special Rules, the acceptance of which was a prerequisite to women's ordination, were a bulwark against any possible future boldness. Though the Eight Special Rules clearly relegated women to a secondary status, Pajapati accepted them in order to achieve her primary goal of establishing an order of nuns.

Later, in a story less frequently told, Pajapati returned with a further request. The implementation of her request would annul the first Special Rule, which required that the most senior nun bow down to even the most novice monk, and thereby would undercut the other seven rules as well:

> "I would ask one thing of the Blessed One, Ananda. It would be good if the Blessed One would allow making salutations, standing up in the presence of another, paying reverence, and the proper performance of duties, to take place equally between both bhikkhus and bhikkhunis according to seniority."
>
> And the venerable Ananda went to the Blessed One [and repeated her words to him].
>
> "This is impossible, Ananda, and I cannot allow it. Even those teachers of false Dharma don't permit such conduct in relation to women; how much less can the Tathagata allow it?"[3]

In Pajapati's attempt to change the first and most blatantly sexist rule, we can understand that she was not in sympathy with the discrimination the rules reflected. Her request also indicates a radical democractic orientation. It comes at a time when even the ancient Greeks, who have been credited with founding democratic rule, only allowed free (i.e., non-slave) males the privilege of citizenship.

Unfortunately, that is all we hear about the politics of the early order of nuns. But we do know a little more about Pajapati. Upon ordination, she received a subject of meditation and through it was able to realize perfection. She writes, "I have reached the state where everything stops," that is *nirodha*, the extinction of senses, feeling, consciousness. This achievement is synonymous with *nirvana*, the highest attainment.

At the ripe old age of one hundred twenty, Pajapati knew that her time of death was near. Though it was against monastic regulations that a sick nun be visited by any monk, Pajapati requested that her son come to her, and by going, the Buddha in effect changed the rule. When she died, miracles occurred both then and at her cremation, which later were said to have been equalled only by those which took place at the Buddha's death.[4] Clearly, the early sangha judged Pajapati to have been a remarkable person.

We can consider Pajapati and her sister Maya, whom Pajapati mentions in the closing stanza of her poem, as the "Great Mothers" of the Buddhist tradition. For Maya, mother of the Buddha, this is an obvious designation. But it is an equally appropriate description of Pajapati, who through countless lives had come to know all relations: mother, son, father, brother, grandmother. Mahapajapati Gotami is clearly an "old soul"; she contains within herself the breadth of experience that makes her the appropriate Founding Mother of Buddhism.

> Homage to you Buddha,
> best of all creatures,
> who set me and many others
> free from pain.
>
> All pain is understood,
> the cause, the craving is dried up,
> the Noble Eightfold Way unfolds,
> I have reached the state where everything stops.
>
> I have been
> mother,
> son,
> father,
> brother,

PARALLAX PRESS

Parallax Press publishes books and tapes on mindful awareness and social responsibility—"making peace right in the moment we are alive." It is our hope that doing so will help alleviate suffering and create a more peaceful world.

For a copy of our free catalogue, please send in this card.

Name _____

Address _____

City _____ State _____ Zip _____

PARALLAX PRESS

P.O. Box 7355

Berkeley, California 94707

grandmother;
knowing nothing of the truth
I journeyed on.

But I have seen the Blessed One;
this is my last body,
and I will not go
from birth to birth
again.

Look at the disciples all together,
their energy,
their sincere effort.
This is homage to the buddhas.

Maya gave birth to Gautama
for the sake of us all.
She has driven back the pain
of the sick and the dying.

PAJAPATI'S DISCIPLES

In one sense, all of the first Buddhist nuns were disciples of Pajapati,
as she was the first ordained nun, the founder of the order, and the
first woman Buddhist teacher. This section will focus only on those
nuns whom we know, from internal evidence in either their story or
poem, to have had a direct connection with Pajapati. These women
fall into several subcategories. There are eight or nine women who
were among the "Five Hundred," the large group which joined
Pajapati in founding the order of nuns. Of these, seven were women
from the harem of Siddhartha Gautama. Also included in this chapter is the story and poem of Pajapati's daughter, Sundari-Nanda and
Pajapati's nurse, Vaddhesi.

THE "FIVE HUNDRED"

The "Five Hundred" were women from the two clans, the Sakyan
and the Koliyan. The Sakyan spoke an Aryan language and claimed
Aryan origins. Their neighbors, the Koliyans, with whom they

shared a common river border, lived a more tribal existence, generally being counted among the aboriginals, with the generic label, "Nagas."

In the first years of the Buddha's teaching career, a bitter struggle broke out between the two clans over the use of the waters of the Rohini River. There was fighting, and some men were killed. In response to this situation, as told in Pajapati's story, Gautama preached a sermon to both factions. The "Five Hundred" were women who had lost their husbands or other male relatives, either in battle or as converts to the Buddha's new teaching. In addition the "Five Hundred" included women of Gautama's harem whom he had left behind at least eleven years before when he renounced his worldly life and took up his spiritual quest.

Several group poems are in the *Therigatha*, but there is no poem attributed to Pajapati's "Five Hundred." However, we do have the story and poem of Mitta.

MITTA

Mitta was one of the "Five Hundred." She was a Sakyan woman from Kapilavatthu, the capital of the Sakyan tribe. Her poem is an appropriate one to introduce the "Five Hundred," because it speaks about the change from lay believer to nun, a change experienced by all these newly ordained women.

In the first stanza of her poem, Mitta speaks as a lay Buddhist; in the second, as a nun. Both the lay and the ordained followed certain rules and observances. For the whole sangha, Uposatha days were a time of special observances, the origins of which go back to Vedic times. These were held on the new, quarter, and full moon, and instead of holding Vedic sacrifices, the Buddhists gave discourses which were open to anyone.[5] Later, the ordained Buddhists observed these days by gathering together to recite the *Patimokkha*, a portion of which follows:

> "Not to do evil, to cultivate good, to purify one's mind, this is the teaching of the buddhas. 'Patience is the highest austerity, forbearance is the highest nibbana,' say the buddhas. One who strikes another is not one who has left home, one who injures another is not an ascetic."[6]

As a lay Buddhist, Mitta would not have participated in the recitation of the *Patimokkha*. The lay observances she describes consisted of keeping the eight precepts (not to be confused with the previously mentioned Eight Special Rules), the sixth of which was eating only one meal a day, before noon, as the ordained did every day.

Mitta appears to have been a devout lay believer, even anxiously so—e.g. "I fasted and fasted." In her case, she didn't find the peace she sought until she became a nun. Her final lines underscore her newfound confidence: "I don't long to be a god. / There is no fear in my heart."

> To be reborn among the gods
> I fasted and fasted
> every two weeks,
> day eight, fourteen, fifteen
> and a special day.
>
> Now with a shaved head
> and Buddhist robes
> I eat one meal a day.
> I don't long to be a god.
> There is no fear in my heart.

THE HAREM

The next group of poems are by women who were members of Siddhartha Gautama's harem. Though it is seldom mentioned, Gautama, besides leaving a wife and child, left a harem of women. Twelve of these women resurface as ones who join Pajapati in founding the community of nuns. Seven of these twelve will be included in this section. Unfortunately, we do not have specific biographical information about any of them—we know only the content of their poems and the general fact that all were Sakyan women. We do know something, however, about marriage and class in that era. We have several legends about the Buddha's harem, and we know about the structure of the harem. This information can help fill out the picture of these women's lives.

According to early Buddhist doctrine, married life was considered inferior to the homeless life of a monk or nun. At the same time, it was acknowledged that not everyone was at the stage of development where she or he could follow the strict discipline of celibacy and renunciation. Marriage was then recommended, and monogamy was the ideal. But, in fact, polygamy and/or extra-marital affairs were the practice of rich and powerful men, Buddhist or otherwise. Such men might be kings, whose harems could be especially large, or they might be wealthy merchants, bankers, or others among the newly emerging, wealthy middle class.

There is a legend about the origin of Gautama's harem. At a special event held on a certain occasion, the young hero Siddhartha was said to have displayed such impressive feats of strength that all the Sakyans sent a daughter to his household, the total number coming to forty thousand! Though this is surely a legend, it was no doubt told to show how powerful a person Siddhartha Gautama was, even in his youth. It was the powerful man's privilege to marry and/or keep more than one woman. For example, Gautama's father, as we know, had two wives; the Buddha's patron and contemporary, King Bimbisara had "five hundred," i.e. many; King Pasenadi also had a number of wives.

Another legend, though it has a misogynist cast, is worth recounting. It shows another motivation behind Siddhartha's renunciation, and in addition, may highlight one stage in a man's psychological journey to maturity. Most of us know the Buddha legend wherein the young, sheltered prince discovers a sick man, an old man, a corpse, and an ascetic. These sights are said to have driven him to plumb the meaning of sickness, old age, and death. But another part of the legend tells of his last night in the palace, when, for the first time, he sees the so-called "real nature of women." His disgust is so thorough that he decides to leave that very night:

> Though the king had heard the determined prince, who was anxious to seek deliverance, he said, "The prince must not go." He ordered additional guards around him and provided him with the most pleasurable of entertainments...
>
> The loveliest of women waited on him... but even music played on instruments like those of the celestial beings failed

to delight him. The ardent desire of that noble prince was to leave the palace in search of the bliss of the highest good.

Whereupon the Akanistha Gods, who excelled in austerities, noting the resolution of the prince, suddenly cast the spell of sleep on the young women, leaving them in distorted postures and shocking poses...

One lay leaning against the side of a window, her slender body bent like a bow, her beautiful necklace dangling...

Another, with loose and disorderly hair, lay like the figure of a woman trampled by an elephant, her ornaments and garments having slipped from her back, her necklace scattered.

And another, of great natural beauty and poise, was shamelessly exposed in an immodest position, snoring out loud, with her limbs tossed about.

Another, with her ornaments and garlands falling off and garments unfastened, lay unconscious like a corpse, with her eyes fixed and their whites showing.

Another with well-developed legs lay as if sprawling in intoxication, exposing what should have been hidden, her mouth gaping wide and slobbering, her gracefulness gone and her body contorted...

Seeing this...the prince was disgusted. "Such is the real nature of women in the world of the living—impure and loathsome, but deceived by dress and ornaments, man is stirred to passion for them."...

Thus arose in the prince a determination to leave that night. The Gods understood his mind and opened the doors of the palace.[7]

The harem consisted of the family of wives, concubines, female relatives and servants associated with a particular man. The institution of the harem can be regarded in several ways. From one perspective we could see it simply and objectively as a social institution of an entirely different culture in which women, though not subject to *purdah* (the seclusion of Indian women of rank after they have attained puberty was a later, Islamic institution of North India), served their master and together lived a domestic life in relative seclusion. From a Western and egalitarian perspective, these women could be called slaves, if by slave we take the common definition of "a person who is the property of and subject to another person, either by capture, purchase, or birth; a person divested of rights."[8]

Within the harem, some were called wives, others consorts. This does not appear to have been a caste distinction, where upper caste women were honored by the title of wife and lower caste women were consorts, concubines, or prostitutes. The story of Khema, whom we will meet in Chapter Three, comes to mind. Although from a ruling family herself, Khema was the "chief consort" of King Bimbisara's harem. It is possible that the distinction between wife and consort was based in part on economics—consorts receiving remuneration, wives not. The *Artha Sastra* speaks of a *ganika* or "chief consort" receiving the very sizable payment of one thousand panas.[9]

Slaves receiving a sizable salary—isn't this a contradiction in terms? Some translators have carefully avoided calling the harem by its name, instead referring to women like Tissa and Sumana as "ladies of the court."[10] Such a rendering of *rajorodha*, (lit., "royal concubine" or "woman of a harem") falsely implies nobility rather than slavery. Even the word consort or concubine fails to convey the degree of subjugation. According to the *Artha Sastra*, the main duties of the harem prostitutes were:

> ...to hold the royal umbrella, golden pitcher and fan, and attend the lord seated in his royal litter, throne or chariot. He could order any of them to surrender herself to anyone to whom he wished to grant a favor, and refusal without just cause entailed a fine.[11]

The penalty for disobedience, cited in another passage of the *Artha Sastra*, was to receive one thousand lashes with a whip.[12]

This gives some background for the seven nuns whose poems follow. The lives of harem women have been summed up in the words of one Indian scholar: "Flocked in a household, they never fared better than cattle, bound in polygamy, such women led a life of abject subservience."[13] Given this as their context, we can see how the Buddha's message of renunciation would have had a special meaning for these former members of the Buddha's harem.

TISSA[14]

Tissa, practice the practice.
Don't let attachments overwhelm you.
Free from ties,
live in the world without obsessions.

SUMANA

Seeing the elements as pain,
don't come back to be born.
When you throw away
your longing to be,
you will live at peace.

UPASAMA

Upasama, you should cross
this flood, this place of death
so hard to cross.
Upasama, you have conquered
Mara and his forces.
Endure this body;
it is your last.

MITTA

Friend,[15]
who has left home in trust,
take delight in friends.
Cultivate good qualities
to gain peace.

VISAKHA

Practice the Buddha's teaching;
you won't regret it!
Right now wash your feet
and sit down beside him.

UTTARA

I was in full possession of
body, speech, and mind.
With the root of craving uprooted,
I have become cool and quenched.

SANGHA

Though we are told that Sangha was a member of Siddhartha's
harem,[16] her poem seems to contradict this. She is a keeper of cows,
thus of the *vaisya* caste, and may have been a farmer's wife.[17] She also
has a child, probably a son, as *putta* most often means "male child."

I gave up my house
and set out into homelessness.
I gave up my child, my cattle,
and all that I loved.
I gave up desire and hate.
My ignorance was thrown out.
I pulled out craving
along with its root.
Now I am quenched and still.

SUNDARI-NANDA

Sundari in Pali means "beautiful," hence, beautiful Nanda. She was
the daughter of Pajapati by Suddhodana, and was considered the
most beautiful woman in her country. But beauty did not seem to be
the most highly valued trait in her family; her half-brother set the
family on a course of religious pursuit that was far more revered.
Therefore, when her brother Nanda, Gautama's son Rahula, and
Pajapati all joined the ordained sangha, and when her father died,
Nanda joined also, not initially out of faith, but out of love for her
kin. Not only was she beautiful, but she shared her half-brother's
natural ability in religious practice, having been declared by him to
be foremost among the nuns in meditative powers.

[Buddha:]
> Nanda,
> look at the body,
> diseased, impure, rotten.
> Focus the mind
> on all this foulness.

(Then the Buddha made an image of a lovely woman
and it aged before Nanda's eyes. He went on:)

> Your body is like this,
> and this is like your body.
> It stinks of decay,
> only a fool would love it.

[Nanda:]
> So day and night
> without letting up,
> I looked at it this way,
> and by my own wisdom,
> I perceived it fully,
> I saw.

> Watching carefully,
> I plumbed to the very origin,
> and saw this body as it really is,
> inside and out.

> Deep inside myself,
> I have lost interest in passion.
> I am careful, quenched,
> calm, and free.

VADDHESI

Vaddhesi was her personal name; her family name is lost. She was
born in Devadaha, the same village as Pajapati, and was Pajapati's
nurse. When Pajapati renounced the world, Vaddhesi did also. We

can assume, therefore, though it is not explicitly stated, that Vaddhesi was among the "Five Hundred." However, when Vaddhesi says, "I went up to a nun I thought I could trust," she is most likely referring to her teacher, Dhammadinna, the eloquent preacher.

Two lists—what Dhammadinna taught her and what Vaddhesi realized—appear in her poem. Some Pali scholars feel that such lists indicate that the poem is likely to have been composed, at least in this form, well after the sixth century B.C.E. They suggest that formulas like those in Vaddhesi's poem show a development from the simplicity of original Buddhist spirituality. This point is debatable; what is certain is that in the early centuries after the first sangha was established, there was a drift towards increasing formalism and dogmatism. Unfortunately, formulas don't easily make for good poetry. What does come through though is Vaddhesi's persistence. Her twenty-five-year stint of miserable failure as a meditator becomes impressive when at last she commits herself wholeheartedly and succeeds.

> It was twenty-five years
> since I left home,
> and I hadn't had a moment's peace.
>
> Uneasy at heart,
> steeped in longing for pleasure,
> I held out my arms and cried out
> as I entered the monastery.
>
> I went up to a nun
> I thought I could trust.
> She taught me the Dharma,
> the elements of body and mind,
> the nature of perception,
> and earth, water, fire, and wind.
>
> I heard her words
> and sat down beside her.

Now I have entered
the six realms of sacred knowledge:
I know I have lived before,
the eye of heaven is pure,
and I know the minds of others.

I have great magic powers
and have annihilated
all the obsessions of the mind.
The Buddha's teaching has been done.

[1] See Appendix 1 for the Eight Special Rules.

[2] This long passage is my adaptation of the *Cullavagga* X, 1, 1-4, from two English translations: Max Müller, ed. *Vinaya Texts*. Translated by T.W. Rhys Davids and Hermann Oldenberg. *Sacred Books of the East*. Vol. XX, Part III. (Oxford: Clarendon Press, 1885), pp. 320-322; and I.B. Horner, tr. *The Book of Discipline*. Vol. V. (London: Luzac and Co., 1952), pp. 352-354.

[3] This is my adaptation of the *Cullavagga* X,3.1. from Max Müller, ed. *Vinaya Texts*. Translated by T.W. Rhys Davids and Herman Oldenberg. *Sacred Books of the East*. Vol. XX, Part III. (Oxford: Clarendon Press, 1885), pp. 327-328.

[4] According to the Buddhist faith, the Buddha did not die. The appropriate concept to express his changed condition is the term, *parinirvana*. It means "full nirvana" and is the extinction of the elements of mind and body, the *skandhas*.

[5] Sukumar Dutt. *Buddhist Monks and Monasteries of India*. (New Delhi: Motilal Banarsidass, 1962), pp. 71-74.

[6] Dutt. *Op. Cit.*, pp. 66-67. The complete *Patimokkha* is found in *Digha Nikaya* 13, verses 181-4.

[7] Theodore du Bary. *The Buddhist Tradition*. (New York: Random House, 1972), pp. 66-67.

[8] *The Compact Edition of the Oxford English Dictionary*. (Oxford: Oxford University Press, 1971), p. 2858.

[9] P. Thomas. *Indian Women Through the Ages*. (Bombay: PS Jayasinghe Asia Publishing House, 1964), p. 71.

[10] Caroline Rhys Davids. *Psalms of the Sisters*. (London: Henry Frowde, Oxford University Press Warehouse, 1909), p. 12.

[11] P. Thomas, *Op. Cit.*, p. 72.

[12] Professor Indra. *Status of Women in Ancient India*. (Varanasi: Motilal Banarasidass, 1955), p. 93.

[13] *Ibid.*, p. 148.

[14] Caroline Rhys Davids has a good note on Tissa: "There is more in this little poem than is at first sight apparent. Tissa—i.e. (a girl) born under the lucky star or constellation of Tissa, a celestial archer (partly identical with Cancer)—suggests a word-play on *tisso sikkhayo*, the three branches of religious training (morals, concentration, insight). Again that a word-play on yoga is intended is intelligible even without the Commentary. 'Let the lucky yoga (conjuncture)—to wit, your rebirth as human, your possession of all your faculties (read *indriya-avekallan*), the advent of a Buddha, your getting conviction—not slip; for by this yoking of opportunities you can free yourself from the four Yokes—viz., sense, renewed existence, opinion, ignorance—which bind you to the wheel of life." *Op. Cit.*, pp. 12-13.

[15] *Mitta* literally means "friend" in Pali.

[16] Rhys Davids. *Op. Cit.*, p. 21.

[17] Dr. Cornelia Dimmitt. "Sanghamitta Day." Lecture given at the Washington D.C. Buddhist Vihara, 1972.

CHAPTER TWO

Patacara & Her Disciples

Patacara was an extraordinary woman, one of the most powerful personalities in the early Buddhist community. Pieces of her history have been lost or confused with those of at least two other nuns, Patacara Pancasata and Kisagotami. We know for a fact that Patacara had a tremendous influence on other nuns, as the poets of the *Therigatha* refer to her more often than to any other woman:

> "I met a nun who had her own food and drink. She was Patacara. She guided me in leaving home, encouraged me, and urged me to the highest goal." (Canda)

> "They stood up, then bowed to her feet. 'We have taken your advice, and will live honoring you.'" (Thirty nuns under Patacara)

> "I went to a nun I thought I could trust." (Uttama)

> "She pulled out the arrow hidden in my heart." (Patacara Pancasta)

We can see from these examples that Patacara was a skillful, revered and charismatic teacher. Women in that era had almost no outlets for self-expression outside the home, and for gifted women like Patacara the existence of an order of nuns enabled them to express their talents in a way that would not have been possible otherwise. Women such as she could exercise a degree of authority, gather and train their own disciples, and also preach to laypeople. And within the community of nuns, such women would be in the company of similarly gifted leaders, like Dhammadinna, Khema, Vasetthi, Uppalavanna, and others.

In this chapter we will consider the poems and stories of Patacara and her circle of disciples, and in Chapter Four we will examine other outstanding women teachers who would have modeled themselves after Patacara, perhaps the finest teacher among them.

PATACARA

Patacara was born into a banker's family in the town of Savatthi. When she was a young woman, her parents arranged for her to marry a young man of equal rank. But one of the family servants was her lover, and, defying her parents' wishes, she ran away with him and set up house in a remote place.

Months passed, and she became pregnant. As her pregnancy came to term, she wanted to go to her parents' home and have their care at the time of birth. Her husband procrastinated, and one day while he was out, she left. He soon discovered what had happened, followed Patacara, and overtook her midway to Savatthi. There, labor came on, she gave birth safely, and together they returned to their dwelling place.

Later, a second child was conceived. Once more Patacara wanted to return to her parents' home, and once more her husband was reluctant. Again she left without him, taking their child, and again he pursued and caught up with her as her labor was beginning. But this time a great storm rose up. Patacara needed shelter, and her husband, while hurriedly cutting grass and stakes in the forest to build a hut, was bitten by a poisonous snake and died. Thinking herself abandoned, Patacara gave birth alone and passed the night lying over her children, using her body to protect them from the storm. In the morning she discovered her husband's body, and she was paralyzed with grief for a day and a night. When the second day dawned, she again took up the journey to her parents' home.

She came to a river swollen with floodwaters. Too weak to carry both children across at once, she took the newborn first. On the far side, she placed the child on a pile of leaves, but was so reluctant to leave him that she looked behind her again and again. Halfway back across the river, she saw a hawk seize her newborn and carry him off. The hawk ignored Patacara's screams, but the older child, thinking his mother was calling him, came up to the riverbank, fell in, and drowned. In utter despair, all Patacara could do was resume her journey.

On the outskirts of Savatthi she met a townsman and asked him whether he knew her family. He said, "Don't ask me about them. Ask about anything else."

"But there is nothing else I care about," she answered.

"You saw how the god rained all last night," he said to her. "Your family's house collapsed and fell on them, and they are all burning on one pyre—the banker, wife, and son. You can see the smoke."

With that, Patacara went out of her mind. She wandered around in circles. Her clothing became ragged and fell off. (Her name, which means "cloak-walker," refers to this.) The townspeople drove her off with sticks and rubbish.

One day, still mad, still walking around in circles, she entered Jeta Grove where the Buddha was preaching. Those who had gathered to listen wanted to keep her away, but Gautama followed her and put himself in her path. As she encountered him, he said, "Sister, recover your presence of mind." And she recovered her presence of mind.

She saw that she was naked. A man threw her his outer robe. "Help me," she said to the Buddha, and she told him her terrible story.

He replied, "Patacara, don't think you have come to someone who can help you. In your many lives, you have shed more tears for the dead than there is water in the four oceans." This made her grief less heavy. He went on to say that when she herself went to another world, no kin could help, that even in this world, no kin can help. And he spoke of the Buddhist path. When he had finished, she asked if she could be ordained. Together they went to the community of nuns, and she was accepted there.

Patacara's poem recounts the moment of her enlightenment experience, which took place later. In one sense this is a type-poem (one of a number of poems that uses the same imagery and theme), playing on the primary meaning of *nirvana*, i.e. the extinguishing of a lamp. Still, few poems in the *Therigatha* are so precise in describing that moment. We see a sequence of events familiar in the Buddhist contemplative tradition—a period of intense concentration, relaxation after that concentration, and a catalyst from outside—the going out of the lamp—that sparks her breakthrough.

> When they plow their fields
> and sow seeds in the earth,

when they care for their wives and children,
young brahmans find riches.

But I've done everything right
and followed the rule of my teacher.
I'm not lazy or proud.
Why haven't I found peace?

Bathing my feet
I watched the bathwater
spill down the slope.
I concentrated my mind
the way you train a good horse.

Then I took a lamp
and went into my cell,
checked the bed,
and sat down on it.
I took a needle
and pushed the wick down.

When the lamp went out
my mind was freed.

THIRTY NUNS UNDER PATACARA

The following poem is one of only three poems in the *Therigatha* attributed to a group of nuns rather than to an individual. Whereas the "Five Hundred" under Mahapajapati (Chapter One) and under Patacara Pancasata (Chapter Five, p. 81) may actually have numbered only fifty or one hundred, the number of nuns indicated in this title may well be accurate.[1] Patacara probably had the largest following of women outside of Pajapati.

This poem of the thirty nuns is modeled after Patacara's poem. The first stanzas of both are similar. The second stanza of the thirty nuns' poem is spoken by Patacara, who is instructing her disciples in correct practice. The second and third stanzas of the thirty nuns' poem speak of bathing the feet. While this was an everyday practice, in this case it appears to be an intentional imitation of the act that preceded Patacara's own enlightenment experience. The fourth stanza of the poem takes the Buddha's enlightenment as its model, and implies that their realization has followed precisely the same pattern as his. In Buddhist religious communities from ancient days to the present, there is a different concept of the individual and of private ownership. There is no such thing as private ownership of religious experience, and, this being the case, imitation is not considered a lack of individual creativity or imagination, but good practice. Hence, stock phrases and even stock stanzas become common teaching devices that bring home the fact that a great teacher's, or the Buddha's, experience is one's own.

[Patacara:]

>With pestles,
>brahmans grind corn.
>Feeding wives and children,
>brahmans find riches.

>"Practice the Buddha's teaching,
>you won't regret it.
>Quickly, when you have washed your feet,
>sit down beside me.
>Intent on peace of mind,
>practice the Buddha's teaching."

[Narrator:]

>When they heard Patacara's teaching
>they washed their feet
>and sat down beside her.
>Intent on peace of mind,
>they practiced the Buddha's teaching.

>In the first watch of the night,
>they remembered they had been born
>before.

In the middle watch of the night,
the eye of heaven became clear.
In the last watch of the night,
the great dark was torn apart.

(They stood up, then bowed to her feet.)

[Thirty Nuns:]
We have taken your advice
and will live honoring you
like the thirty gods honoring Indra
who never lost a battle.

We have the three knowledges.
There are no obsessions in our minds.

CANDA

Canda was another of the nuns who turned to the Buddha's path after great personal loss and suffering. Though originally she belonged
to a rich family, her family lost all its wealth and possessions while
she was still a child. Later their village was wracked by a mysterious
plague. Called *ahiwataka-roga* ("snake-blast disease"[2]) because it was
believed to take the form of a blast from the breath of poisonous serpents, it would come at the season of the year when the flies first die
off, presumably late summer. The initial victims would be lizards and
other reptiles, then larger animals like cats, dogs, and goats, and finally humans would fall ill and die. Canda's parents, husband, and
children died; of her entire family, only she survived. To make mat-
ters still worse, without relatives she was unable to support herself,
and was forced to beg from house to house for food.

In this condition, it is remarkable that Canda should have encountered Patacara, who by this time had become a renowned nun
and teacher. While their particular situations had been different, the
loss of all family through tragic circumstances made their stories very
similar. Fully able to empathize with Canda's wretchedness, Patacara
gave her food and taught her dharma. And Canda, astonished, became her disciple.

I was in a bad way,
a widow,
no children, no friends,
no relations to give me food and clothes.

I was a beggar with a bowl and stick
and wandered
house to house
in the heat and cold
for seven years.

But I met a nun
who had food and drink,
and I went up to her and said,
"Take me into the homeless life."

She was Patacara.
Out of pity she guided me
in leaving home,
encouraged me,
and urged me to the highest goal.

I took her advice.
It wasn't wasted.

I have the three knowledges.[3]
There are no obsessions in my mind.

UTTAMA

Uttama also came from a banker's family in Savatthi. Meeting Patacara was a turning point in her life, and she became a nun. However, Uttama had a lot of difficulty making progress on the path. Perceiving her confusion, Patacara was able to utter some words (the original text says it was this poem itself) which gave Uttama an opening, and subsequently led to her enlightenment.

In the *Satipatthana Sutra* the Buddha says that if any person practices the Dharma for seven years, or seven months, or seven weeks, or even for seven days, with the utmost resolution and sincerity, highest knowledge here and now is possible.[4] In her poem, Uttama refers to this idea specifically as she describes her subsequent enlightenment.

> Four or five times
> I left my cell.
> I had no peace of mind,
> no control over my mind.
>
> I went to a nun
> I thought I could trust.
> She taught me the Dharma,
> the elements of body and mind,
> the nature of perception,
> and earth, water, fire, and wind.
>
> I heard what she said
> and sat cross-legged
> seven days full
> of joy.
>
> When, on the eighth
> I stretched my feet out,
> the great dark was torn apart.

---

[1] The Indian scholar Kosambi suggests that the total number of Buddhist disciples at the time of the Buddha's *parinirvana* probably numbered less than five hundred [D.D. Kosambi. *Ancient India*. (New York: World Publishing Co., 1969), p. 106]; on the other hand, there is some evidence in the Pali Canon that suggests a greater following. For example, 1250 disciples are said to have gathered on one Maga Puja full moon ceremony.

[2] R.S. Hardy. *Eastern Monachism*. (London: Partridge and Oakey, 1850), p. 85.

[3] This is translated from the Pali *te-vijja* (lit. "the three knowledges"). In Brahman the term means "knowledge of the three vedas."

[4] T.W. Rhys Davids, ed. *The Digha Nikaya. Vol. II*. (London: published for the Pali Text Society by Henry Frowde, 1903), pp. 290-315, and Lord Chalmers, tr. *Further Dialogues of the Buddha*. 2 Volumes. (London: Oxford University Press, 1927), p. 41.

CHAPTER THREE

Wanderers & Disciples

This chapter is comprised of an eclectic group of unconventional women who were wanderers, ascetics, novices, ordained nuns, hermits, almswomen, and disciples. These were women who, while not renowned as teachers or preachers, were nonetheless exceptional for their independence of thought and action. This chapter will consider this colorful and diverse group in terms of two specific attributes: wandering (homelessness) and discipleship. In a sense, all of the women of the *Therigatha*, as disciples of the Buddha, could be included in this chapter. The ones here have been selected because the themes of wandering and discipleship are emphasized in their stories or poems.

WANDERERS

The Sanskrit and Pali languages supply us with abundant evidence that women filled a wide variety of unconventional roles. *Manavika* is a term for a female student in an ascetic order; *samani*, a female renunciant or recluse; *cariki*, a female wanderer;[1] *brahmacarini*, a female student under Brahmanism; *sikkhamana*, a female Buddhist probationer (there is no male equivalent for this term); *bhikkhuni*, a Buddhist nun who has completed twelve years as an ordained nun; *theri*, a Buddhist female elder; *paribbajika*, a female ascetic; *molibaddha-paribbajika*, a female ascetic who has her hair tied up in a top-knot; *komara-brahmacariya*, a woman who practices the vow of celibacy. The Greek traveler, Megasthenes, who visited India at the time of Chandra Gupta Maurya (around the third century B.C.E.), mentions female wanderers who studied philosophy and abstained from sexual intercourse.[2]

These women followed the ancient tradition of the *pabbajita*,[3] "the wanderer," or "one who has set out from home into homelessness." That the word also occurs in the feminine form (*pabbajitâ*) indicates that women also led this life. The *Digha Nikaya* reveals the existence of sixty-two heresies and wandering communities.[4] Jain texts likewise lend support to the existence of such communities.

Women as well as men supported many of these heresies, if not always actively participating, by supporting with alms those mendicants who did.

In the very first years following the formation of the Buddhist order, the solitary life was highly esteemed. The *muni*, "sage" exemplified this ideal. The *Sutta Nipata* does not mention female *muni* in its description of the *muni* phase. However, solitude was not a necessary prerequisite for leading the religious life. Setting out into homelessness did not automatically mean going into isolation from other people. As pointed out in the *Vanapattha Sutta*, the renunciant "may dwell in the forest or quit it, or dwell anywhere in a village, township, or a country according as such dwelling is conducive to his or her spiritual cultivation or not."[5] Whether living in solitude or in the company of others, the ideal common to all wanderers was the renunciation of the home-life for the sake of a higher spiritual life.

By renouncing motherhood and acting independently, the wandering women renunciants challenged two fundamental beliefs about women in early Indian society. Thus, in many respects, female wanderers were often equated with "loose women"—prostitutes, actresses, dancers and musicians—women who did not have an active male guardian and moved relatively freely in the public sphere. While on the surface, a greater contrast between the "loose woman" and the renunciant is hard to conceive, yet they did have one thing in common: their unwillingness to accept the conventional roles of wife and mother and submit to the authority of father, husband, and son as prescribed by writers in the Smriti period (400-700 C.E.), like Manu, who codified ancient Indian laws.

> By a girl, by a young woman, or even by an aged one, nothing must be done independently. In childhood, a female must be subject to her father, in youth to her husband, when her lord is dead to her sons; a woman must never be independent.[6]

Although the strict discipline of the Buddhist nuns' sangha and the Eight Special Rules attempted to guarantee the good reputation of the women renunciant, both Buddhist and Jain rules attest to the fact that unattached women were vulnerable. Brahmanic legislation held various crimes—especially sexual offenses against an actor's wife or daughter, women who made their living through "exploits," or female ascetics—as equivalent before the law but less severely punishable than those committed against other women.[7]

Perhaps gathering into groups was for protection. In any case, neophytes especially attached themselves to a teacher and practiced their teaching. The young Siddhartha Gautama took this route of studying under a number of teachers—his first teacher was a woman ascetic. So too, Bhadda Kundalekesa, from this chapter, attached herself to a series of teachers of Jain and other persuasions, mastering the teachings of each as she went. We should remember that this was a time before universities and before there were such things as teachers in residence. At most, one might find an early forest school where classes were held under trees, and male and female students tended cattle and did open-air exercises.[8] But generally those who yearned for knowledge wandered. And if two wanderers met, the customary questions they exchanged were, "Who is your teacher?" and "What is his or her teaching?"

The origins of the *pabbajita* tradition are not clear. One certainty is that the origins are not Aryan, as the Vedas unwaveringly upheld the religiosity of the householder. Some of the *Upanishads*, the most ancient of which predate the Buddha's lifetime by at least a century, depict the beginnings of a movement within Brahmanism that turned away from the household life and idealized the renunciants as "those who live in the forests purified by austerities, those who know and are learned."[9] That this ideal is found in the earliest *Upanishads* suggests a pre-Upanidhadic origin, and yet there is no prototype for the renunciant in the *Vedas*. If we go back to a time even before the *Vedas*, we find iconography of male renunciants from the Indus civilization cities of Harappa and Mohenjodaro. This suggests the ideal of renunciation to be truly ancient.[10]

Rarely, however, in any of these literary and iconographic records of early Indian culture do we discover depictions of women renunciants—none at all in the Indus iconography, none in the *Vedas*, and only a few in the *Upanishads*. The poems in this section therefore represent the earliest body of evidence which indicates women's participation in the *pabbajita* tradition. The absence of earlier records is not proof in itself that women did not seek truth in a mode that was available as far back as such wisdom-traditions extended. Though we cannot trace their histories, we can have no doubt that they existed, if for no other reason than that the yearning for knowledge is timeless and transcends gender.

BUDDHIST WOMEN DISCIPLES

Although the tradition of female mendicancy continued from the early Vedic period to the Buddhist age, records from the pre-Buddhist period tell us only of exceptional individuals, not of whole bands, communities, or organizations of women. Buddhist monasticism added the idea of an organized community of nuns to this tradition. It was not a completely novel ideal. Mahavira, the Jain leader, had already allowed for the formation of a sangha of nuns, some thirty-six thousand women becoming nuns under the Svetambara sect of the Jain order. But under Buddhism, more women still were prepared to renounce worldly ties than ever before.

There is no question that the women who chose to join the Buddhist sangha were going against prevailing social norms. The fact that unprecedented numbers of women were making this choice was disturbing to orthodox Aryans, who had very definite and conservative ideas about a woman's place. It is possible that women who entered the Buddhist sangha were thought incapable of having children, and therefore, better monastic than marital risks. To disprove this possibility and demonstrate that women candidates actively chose the homeless life rather than being forced into it for want of other options, only healthy, physiologically "normal" women were permitted to join the sangha. The predominant organ, the health of which preoccupied the senior male and female preceptors, was the uterus. Of the twenty-four reasons for disqualification, eleven were concerned with "abnormalities, deformities or diseases, all of which have reference to the womb or its accessories."[11] Some of them, say translators T.W. Rhys Davids and H. Oldenberg, "are unintelligible to us."[12] Even without a complete list of the disqualifications, it is safe to conclude that aspiring women disciples needed to demonstrate uterine normality.

An even more threatening possibility was that a nun might possess special powers or knowledge pertaining to childbearing, either

as a midwife or as an abortionist. Bloomfield mentions that evil female ascetics were known to have sometimes been "engaged in independent magic practices, but this field is, in the main, pre-empted
by witches."[13] In Buddhist literature there is the story of a woman
who, having become pregnant by her lover, asked a Buddhist nun, a
friend of hers, to carry away the fetus in her alms-bowl. Whether this
nun was acting as an abortionist or not is unclear. What is clear is
that abortion was regarded as the most heinous of crimes among ancient Indians, perhaps especially so among the Buddhists, whose first
precept was against the taking of life. It was considered a form of
murder to give medicines to a woman or "suggest…methods such as
rubbing the abdomen or fomenting it, etc. to bring about abortion."[14]

The occasional story or passage about a Buddhist nun engaged in
childbirth, magical practices, or abortion, is rare in the Pali literature. Of greater concern to the women, indeed the purpose for which
they had joined the sangha, was religious realization. As ordination
was seen as the route to that accomplishment, religious realization,
not magic or the practices surrounding conception, birth, or contra-
ception, was the subject of outstanding interest. No subject in the
Bhikkhunivibhanga, the "Nun's Book of Discipline," is given a comparable degree of attention.

By reading the *Bhikkhunivibhanga* closely, we can discern the stages
of development in the life of the Buddhist woman disciple. The first
step in the ordination process was *pabbajja,* setting out from home
into homelessness. In this first stage, a woman could choose to be a
probationer (*sikkhamana*). In contrast to the male novice, the female
probationer was an entrant with distinct duties and responsibilities.
She would observe the first five precepts (*silas*),[15] incumbent on all
Buddhist disciples, lay or ordained, plus the sixth precept of abstain-
ing from eating at the wrong time. She had to be at least twenty
years of age.[16] She had to have the consent of her parents or husband, as well as the consent of both the nuns' and the monks'
sangha. It does not seem to have been compulsory for the woman to
sever all ties with the world in this stage. She did not have to reject
the company of men. The actual religious instruction given to the
female probationers and nuns was not different than that imparted
to their male counterparts.

The next stage of discipleship a woman could choose was ordination. After a female probationer had trained for two years under a senior nun, she was eligible for ordination. It was the sangha, not the training nun, who made the decision to accept the candidate. Whereas the male candidate needed acceptance only from the monks' sangha, the female candidate needed to be accepted by both the nuns' and the monks' sangha. Hence, the ordination ceremony for the female candidate involved two phases. Though the actual ordination was the same in both sanghas, the nuns "raised her up" (*vutthapeti*), and the monks "ordained her fully" (*upasampadeti*).

While *bhikkhuni* was the commonly used term for a nun, it technically implied a further stage in the disciple's development. Technically a *bhikkhuni* was a nun who had been ordained for twelve years. After completing twelve years, a nun could ask the order for the privilege of conferring ordination (*vutthapana*—the ability to confer ordination). This would make her a training nun (*upajjha*).

These are the main stages of a woman disciple's development in terms of the monastic organization. It should be understood that these stages were independent of special abilities and attainments such as preaching, psychic powers, or arahantship. Previous to the rise of Buddhist monastic organization, in the very earliest days of the sangha (or in the case of exceptional disciples like Baddha Kundalakesa), the Buddha simply said "*ehi*" ("come") to confer ordination.

BHADDA KUNDALAKESA

Bhadda was born into a financier's family in Rajagaha. One day, as a young woman sitting at her window, she saw a highway robber being led to execution. Falling in love with him at first sight, she begged her father to obtain his release. Out of a misguided love he did, bribing the guards heavily. Then he had the man bathed, dressed in fine clothes, and brought before her.

The robber's name was Satthuka, and he was the son of a king's minister. Despite his prestigious family background and this opportunity for a new beginning, he remained true to his former trade; he was less interested in Bhadda's love than in the jewels she wore. So he made up this story—when the city guards were leading him to

Robber's Cliff for execution, he had vowed to the cliff deity that if he were spared, he would return and make an offering.

Bhadda prepared such an offering, and together they went to the cliff, at his request, leaving her attendants behind. But when they were alone and he showed neither affection nor gratitude, she began to be afraid.

At the summit of the cliff he said, "Do you really think I have come here to make an offering? What a fool you are! I have come for your jewels." And he ordered her to remove her outer robe and wrap her jewels inside.

Without hesitation she replied, "Please grant me one wish," and she asked if she could embrace him once before she died. He agreed, and she embraced him first from the front. Then, embracing him from the back, she pushed him over the cliff. For this act, even the deity of the cliff applauded her, praising her keen presence of mind, and saying:

> Wisdom is not always confined to men;
> A woman, too, is wise, and shows it now and then.[17]

Afterwards, Bhadda could not face her family. She chose to enter the order of the Svetambara Jains, the first religious sect in history to establish an order of nuns. Asked what level of renunciation she wished to undertake, Bhadda said that she wanted to commit herself to their severest asceticism. Therefore, in one of the austerities of initiation, they tore out her hair.[18] Eventually, she mastered all the Jain teachings, but grew dissatisfied and left that sangha, traveling here and there in search of the wisest teachers.

Whenever Bhadda arrived in a new village her method of announcing her desire to engage in religious debate was to stick a rose-apple branch in a pile of sand. The village children kept watch on that branch to see if anyone would challenge her by knocking it down. If the branch withered while she remained at a village, she would procure a fresh one. After years of this kind of "dharma-encounter," Bhadda could find no equal.

Then one day she came to Savatthi and stuck a rose-apple branch in a pile of sand. Gautama's leading disciple, Sariputta, lived in Savatthi, and noticing the branch, he requested that some children knock it down. The debate thus established, a crowd of villagers gathered. Bhadda put her questions first, but Sariputta could answer them all with ease, even the most abstruse. Then came his turn and he asked her, "One—what is that?" Bhadda paused, and, not knowing how to respond, asked that he become her teacher. Instead, Sariputta sent her to Gautama, who recognized her depth of understanding and gave her instruction. Hearing his words, she attained immediate enlightenment. Then, in a rare gesture of respect, the Buddha ordained her by simply saying, "Come, Bhadda."

Of this unique ordination, Isabel Horner writes,

> When female novices wished to receive the Upasampada ordination, they had to ask for it from both the Sanghas [the sangha of nuns and of monks]. Only one kind of exception to this custom was known, and that was when Gautama himself ordained an entrant by saying, 'Come,' calling the entrant by name. This kind of ordination is recorded of one woman, Bhadda Kundalakesa, the ex-Jain.[19]

Gautama considered Bhadda first among the nuns in the speed with which she gained *nirvana*. But we should not overlook the years of experience that preceded that realization.

In her poem, Bhadda tells of her former austere practices and then of her life as a Buddhist almswoman. Even after her conversion to Buddhism, she seems to have kept her independent, wandering ways. This detail associates her with the very earliest days of the Buddhist sangha, when nuns were still permitted the freedom of solitary wandering.

> I cut my hair and wore the dust,
> and I wandered in my one robe,
> finding fault where there was none,
> and finding no fault where there was.
>
> Then I came from my rest one day
> at Vulture Peak
> and saw the pure Buddha
> with his monks.

I bent my knee,
paid homage,
pressed my palms together.
We were face to face.

"Come, Bhadda," he said;
that was my ordination.

I have wandered throughout
Anga and Magadha,
Vajji, Kasi, and Kosala;
fifty-five years with no debt,
I have enjoyed the alms of these kingdoms.

A wise lay follower
gained a lot of merit;
he gave a robe to Bhadda
who is free from all bonds.

NANDUTTARA

Nanduttara was of a brahman family. She lived in the kingdom
of the Kurus, in the town of Kammasadamma. Like Bhadda
Kundalakesa, Nanduttara first joined the order of the Jains. Also like
Bhadda, she became renowned and traveled around India with a
rose-apple bough in hand, challenging anyone to religious debate.

Just as Bhadda had met her match in Sariputta, Nanduttara met
hers in Moggallana. Gautama described these monks as twin broth-
ers and as his two most eminent disciples:

> Sariputta is as she who brings forth, Moggallana is as the nurse
> of what is brought forth; Sariputta trains in the fruit of con-
> version, Moggallana trains in the highest good.[20]

Nanduttara entered into debate with Moggallana and, convinced
of the power of his insight, became converted to Buddhism and
swiftly realized its highest goal.

In the first two stanzas of her poem, Nanduttara compares the superficially opposed life-styles she has led in the past. In the first

stanza, she practices the rituals of the brahmans, worshipping the fire god Agni. In the next stanza, she is still caught up in her upper-class origins, but instead, devotion is to her body and its lovely appearance. When she "sees the body as it really is," she realizes that both of these former ways are simply two aspects of the same misunderstanding. That brand of religious devotion and/or sensuality, by externalizing faith, has obscured it. With this realization, she comes to a new freedom.

> I used to worship fire,
> the moon, the sun,
> and the gods.
> I bathed at fords,
> took many vows,
> I shaved half my head,
> slept on the ground,
> and did not eat after dark.
>
> Other times
> I loved make-up and jewelry,
> baths and perfumes,
> just serving my body
> obsessed with sensuality.
>
> Then faith came.
> I took up the homeless life.
> Seeing the body as it really is,
> desires have been rooted out.
>
> Coming to birth is ended
> and my cravings as well.
> Untied from all that binds
> my heart is at peace.

DANTIKA

Dantika was from Savatthi, the daughter of a minister of the King of Kosala. She joined the community of nuns under Pajapati. In

her poem, the lovely closing line, "I went into the forest and concentrated my mind," connects her with the earliest followers of
Gautama, as it was particularly among them that the life of the for-
est-dwelling renunciant was extolled. In that age, virgin forest covered a great portion of the land surrounding the Ganges River,
separating the towns by great distances. Wandering ascetics and yo-
gis who went into the forest for solitude were also supported by the
forest; they slept under trees and ate wild foods. "Some followers of
the Sakyan [Gautama] dwelt in forests, there to subsist on fruit and
roots and to dress in bark and antelope's hides."[21] For this reason it
has been suggested that the emerging Buddhist movement, in common with the whole tradition of wandering renunciants, constituted
a return to the old ways of the food gathers, the aboriginal forest
dwellers.[22]

Dantika went to the forest to carry out her meditation undis-
turbed. But perhaps she dwelt there as well. References to the solitary life are rare in the poems of the nuns. Some of the early nuns
who lived in the forest as hermits were raped, and because of this, it
became a rule of the sangha that women could no longer go into the
forest alone.[23] Dantika's poem may predate this rule.

> As I left my daytime resting place on
> Vulture Peak,
> I saw an elephant
> come up on the riverbank
> after its bath.
>
> A man took a hook and said to the
> elephant,
> "Give me your foot."
> The elephant stretched out its foot;
> the man mounted.
>
> Seeing what was wild before
> gone tame under human hands,
> I went into the forest
> and concentrated my mind.

SAKULA

Sakula came from Savatthi and was a member of the brahman caste. It was in her town that an important Buddhist monastery was established in the beautiful park, Jeta Grove. This grove was the gift of a kind and devout lay follower named Anathapindika, and Sakula was present on that occasion. The ceremony of dedication for the new monastery was one of great splendor. Hundreds of distinguished people attended and the festivities lasted nine months.

During this time, Sakula decided to become a lay disciple. Still, she was uneasy about her life, and after hearing an enlightened monk speak, she decided to become a nun. Not only did she become an arahant later on, but she was singled out by Gautama as foremost among the nuns possessing the psychic power of the "eye of heaven," the ability to see into all worlds, near and far.

Many poems of the *Therigatha* and *Theragatha* highlight one Buddhist concept or another, but Sakula's poem is an important one in that it incorporates a number of key ideas. In the first stanza, Sakula speaks as a laywoman who, through the preaching of a monk, learns of *nirvana*. (The word *nirvana*, *nibbana* in Pali, has been left untranslated.) In the second stanza, Sakula has become a Buddhist nun. She tells us what she has had to leave behind in order to take up this path—a son and a daughter, money and grain. In the third stanza, Sakula speaks of her achievement of cutting out desire and hatred—the so-called "marks of existence"—and of eliminating the *asavas*, the obsessions of the mind. In the fourth stanza, Sakula attains the first two of the three knowledges, remembrance of former lives and the "eye of heaven," the psychic ability to see things near and far. In the final stanza, she tells of her insight into the impermanence of all conditioned existence, reiterates that she has eliminated the mind's obsessions, and closes with the stock phrase—"I am quenched and cool."

> When I lived in a house
> I heard a monk's words
> and saw in those words
> nirvana
> the unchanging state.

I am the one
who left son and daughter,
money and grain,
cut off my hair,
and set out into homelessness.

Under training
on the straight way,
desire and hatred fell away,
along with the obsessions
of the mind
that combine with them.

After my ordination,
I remembered
I had been born before.
The eye of heaven became clear.

The elements of body and mind
I saw as other,
born from a cause,
subject to decay.
I have given up the obsessions
of the mind.
I am quenched and cool.

SIHA

Siha was the niece of Sihasenapati, a famous general of the Licchavis. Sihasenapati had been a follower of the Jain sect, but when he met Gautama, he converted to Buddhism. His niece was named after him; her name means "lioness." She grew up in Vesali and, hearing Gautama preach one day, she decided to enter the nuns' order. For the next seven years she sincerely followed the Buddhist path but "without having attained peace of mind at any time." Reaching a point of despair, she resolved to kill herself. The result of her attempted suicide was not death but a deep religious experience and a new beginning.

We know that near-death experiences are frequently accompanied by religious experiences. With the pioneering work of Dr. Elizabeth Kübler-Ross, this fact is increasingly acknowledged in scientific circles:

> We've had people who had no vital signs who describe watching the scene, the hospital room, the accident scene, from a distance. They were very peaceful and serene while they observed. In the near-death experience, the body becomes perfect again. Quadriplegics are no longer paralyzed, multiple-sclerosis patients who have been in wheelchairs for years say that when they were out of their bodies, they were able to sing and dance.[24]

Siha's own near-death experience might have had some of the qualities that Dr. Kübler-Ross describes. Her breakthrough may have had elements of peace, serenity, and of the body and mind being perfect. Returning to her community afterwards, Siha must have lived at a deeper level because of the experience.

> Obsessed by sensuality
> I never got to the origin,
> but was agitated,
> my mind beyond control.
>
> I dreamed of a great happiness.
> I was passionate
> but had no peace.
>
> Pale and thin
> I wandered seven years,
> unhappy day and night.
>
> Then, I took a rope into the forest
> and thought
> I'd rather hang than go back
> to that narrow life.

I tied a strong noose
to the branch of a tree
and put it round my neck—
just then my heart was set free!

ANOTHER UTTAMA

We have already met one Uttama among Patacara's disciples. A second woman by that same name came from a brahman family of Kosala. Uttama heard Gautama when he was preaching in her area and joined the sangha. Afterwards, she spoke this poem, declaring her attainment. She describes this event in terms of the Seven Factors of Enlightenment: concentration, energy, rapture, investigation, tranquility, equanimity, and mindfulness. This first stanza is identical to that of Jenti's poem in Chapter Eight.

The Buddha taught
Seven Factors of Enlightenment.
They are ways to find peace
and I have developed them all.

I have found what is vast and empty,
the unborn.
It is what I've longed for.
I am a true daughter of the Buddha,
always finding joy
in peace.

I have ended the hunger
of gods and humans,
and I will not wander
from birth to birth.
I have no thought of becoming.

MITTAKALI

Mittakali's decision to enter the order came when she heard Gautama preach the *Maha Satipatthana Sutta*.[25] This scripture, recited to this day in Theravadin monasteries in Southeast Asia, is considered by many to be the most important discourse given by the Buddha on meditation practice. Until this point in her life, Mittakali had the reputation of being a difficult person, angry and self-centered. Hearing this, she changed, putting great effort into her new life. Gradually her insight deepened, and she became an arahant.

Mittakali's poem is fascinating because, like Patacara's poem, it describes the precise moment of her realization experience. Poems like these are gems of Pali literature. Patacara says, "The lamp went out. / My mind was freed." For Mittakali, "I stood up. / My mind was completely free." In both cases, realization follows an experience of personal disappointment or fear. For Patacara, "But I've done everything right / and followed the rule of my teacher. / Why haven't I found peace?" For Mittakali, "I lost my way. / My passions used me / and I forgot the real point / of my wandering life...there was only terror." Yet another similarity between these two enlightenment poems is that their experiences are both characterized by insight into impermanence. According to the *Therigatha* Commentary, for Patacara it was watching water trickling from high to low ground and then disappearing that led her to see the transitory nature of all life. For Mittakali, it was seeing the *skandhas*—the elements of mind and body, rising and falling away—that led her to recognize things as they really are, impermanent.

> Although I left home for no home
> and wandered, full of faith,
> I was still greedy
> for possessions and praise.
>
> I lost my way.
> My passions used me,
> and I forgot the real point
> of my wandering life.
>
> Then as I sat in my little cell,
> there was only terror.
> I thought—this is the wrong way,
> a fever of longing controls me.

Life is short.
Age and sickness gnaw away.
I have no time for carelessness
before this body breaks.

And as I watched the elements of mind and body
rise and fall away
I saw them as they really are.
I stood up.
My mind was completely free.
The Buddha's teaching has been done.

[1] Mary E. Lilly. *Theri Apadana of the Khuhhakanikaya*. Part II. (London: published for the Pali Text Society by Oxford University Press, 1927), p. 519.

[2] Meena Talim. *Women in Early Buddhist Literature*. (Bombay: University of Bombay, 1972), p. 1.

[3] Sukumar Dutt. *Buddhist Monks and Monasteries of India*. (Delhi: Motilal Banarsidass, 1962), pp. 37-42.

[4] Meena Talim, *Op. Cit.*, p. 1.

[5] *Majjhima Nikaya*. No. 17. Vanapattha Sutta.

[6] *Laws of Manu*: v. 147-148 or Katherine Marsh, "The Theriigatha and the Theraagatha." Mimeographed thesis. (Cornell University, 1980), p. 8.

[7] Katherine Marsh. *Op. Cit.*, p. 10.

[8] Hari Ramchandra Wekar. *Women in Ancient India*. (Kasturba Indore, India: Kasturba Gandhi National Memorial Trust, 1962), pp. 36-37.

[9] Sukamar Dutt. *Buddhist Monks and Monasteries in India*. (Delhi: Motilal Banarsidass, 1962), pp. 37-38.

[10] J. Marshall. *Mohenjodaro and Indus Civilization*. Vol. I. (London: Probsthain, 1931), pp. 53-56.

[11] Katherine Marsh. *Op Cit.*, p. 15.

[12] *Ibid.*, p. 15.

[13] Maurice Bloomfield. "False Ascetics and Nuns in Hindu Fiction." *JAOS* 44: 202-42.

[14] *Ibid.*, p. 16

[15] The five *silas* or Buddhist precepts are (1) not to kill, (2) not to steal, (3) to refrain from sexual misconduct, (4) not to lie, and (5) not to give or use intoxicants.

[16] For a discussion of the age of female entrants, see the introduction to I.B. Horner. *The Book of Discipline. (Suttavibhanga)* Vol I. (London: Oxford University Press Warehouse, 1938).

[17] E.W. Burlingame. *Buddhist Legends: The Dhammadapa Commentary.* Harvard Oriental Series, Vol. 28.(Cambridge: Harvard University Press, 1921), p. 229.

[18] This is the practice of *loya*, "uprooting the hair from the head." See S.C. Deo. *History of Jaina Monachism.* (Poona: Deccan College, 1956).

[19] I. B. Horner. *Women Under Primitive Buddhism.* (London: George Routledge and Sons, Ltd., 1930. Reprinted by Asia Books Corp., 1975), pp. 213-214.

[20] Richard Morris, ed. *Buddhavamsa.* Commentary 31 (London: Henry Frowde Oxford University Press Warehouse, 1882).

[21] I.B. Horner, trans. *The Book of Discipline (Suttavibhanga)* Vol. I. (London: Oxford University Press Warehouse, 1938), p. xxix.

[22] D.D. Kosambi. *Ancient India.* (New York: World Publishing Co., 1969), p. 104.

[23] Max Müller, ed. *Vinaya Texts.* Translated by T.W. Rhys Davids and Hermann Oldenberg. *Sacred Books of the East.* Vol. XX Part III. (Oxford: Clarendon Press, 1885), pp. 362-363. Reprinted by Delhi Motilal Banarsidass, 1969.

[24] Elizabeth Kübler-Ross. "Interview." *Playboy* (August, 1981), pp. 86-87.

[25] *Digha Nikaya* No. 22. *Majjhima Nikaya* No. 10.

CHAPTER FOUR

Wise Women & Teachers

In Chapters One and Two we met Mahapajapati and Patacara, the two most revered Buddhist women. In this chapter we will consider a number of other Buddhist nuns who were renowned as wise women and teachers. Coming from a society in which women were expected to be wives and mothers, courtesans and prostitutes, it is striking to discover women in the sixth century B.C.E. respected for their spiritual realization.

Religious realization in ancient India was an achievement gained by arduous cultivation of the body and mind. Buddhists called those who had attained the highest realization *arahants*, literally, "holy ones." The Jains also used this term. The brahmans referred to their religious sages as *brahmana*, to their priests and seers of special authority as *rishi*. This chapter uses the phrase "wise women," not found in Pali texts, to draw attention to some examples of women who have pursued the Buddhist path to complete realization. In an environment in which there were few precursors and few structures that supported the cultivation of religious mastery, these wise women had taken an important step. Women teachers carried their accomplishment one step further by communicating their understanding to others.

In the pre-Buddhist period, we find occasional references to *rishikas* and *brahmavadinis*, women seers and sages. Because such references are rare, these women seem like meteors, coming out of nowhere and disappearing with no apparent trace. But indeed, there had been some tradition of wise women and teachers, though most of the names of actual women and details of that tradition are obscured or lost. Women do not become religious teachers in a vacuum, but rather in a cultural context that supports their achievement. In order to understand the context in which the women of the *Therigatha* could attain the highest goals of their religious system and teach that path to others, we must understand something of their cultural inheritance and the position and status of women in ancient Indian society.

The Aryan incursion into India about 1500 B.C.E.[1] succeeded in imposing a patriarchal order and predominantly male pantheon on the formerly matriarchal society of the Indus valley.[2] Surprisingly, this period of upheaval, the spirit of which is captured in the figure of the warrior god Indra, was one in which the position of women was comparatively good. Economically, women made valuable contributions, participating in agricultural work, making clothes, baskets, and arrows. In the religious sphere, too, women had a fair degree of equal opportunity. Girls, like boys, were initiated at puberty, after which they could study the sacred texts, the *Vedas*, which harked back to the period of conquest in the Punjab of northwestern India. Not only did initiated women receive a religious education, but they were able to share in Vedic rituals with their husbands, and unmarried women could also offer sacrifices. However, this relatively privileged status applied only to women belonging to the higher castes. Neither a *sudra* wife—*sudra* being the lowest caste (servants or slaves)—nor a wife purchased by bride price, was entitled to any religious rights or privileges.[3]

Some women became poets, scholars, and teachers. That women made major contributions in the intellectual and religious spheres can be inferred from the fact that certain hymns of the *Rig Veda* are attributed to female *rishis*. These include hymns entirely or partly attributed to *rishikas*, and those attributed to *rishikas* but of dubious authorship. According to Indian tradition, Apala, Vishvavara, and Ghoaa were authors of *Rig Veda* hymns, and other hymns are ascribed to goddesses, mortal women, and abstract feminine essences, including Lopamudra, Shashiyasi, Indrani, Urvashi, Yami, Surya, Sanchi, and some twenty others.[4]

In the period from 1000 to 500 B.C.E., Aryan political expansion was complete and included the Ganges as well as the Indus valleys. As a significant segment of the native Dravidian population had become *sudra*, and as a large pool of cheap or unpaid labor became readily available, women's work became less valued. Women no longer participated in agriculture, a mainstay of the economy, but were restricted to home and cottage industries. In addition, intermarriage and/or intermixture of Aryan men with non-Aryan women lowered the status of women generally. During this same period, Brahmanic sacred texts became increasingly esoteric, and ritual and sacrifice grew so complicated that a longer course of study was required. Fewer women could devote themselves to this study. Increasingly, girls' initiations were abandoned and women's participation in sacrifices became a formality.

Because the Brahmanic culture was less and less supportive of women's efforts to gain an education, the few examples of women who gained access to esoteric knowledge or who became teachers are all the more noteworthy. The two best-known examples of *brahmavadinis* are Gargi and Maitreyi. Both lived in the ninth century B.C.E. Gargi was of an equal age and social status as the great sage Yajnavalkya, and may have studied in the same *ashram* as he. At a religious assembly, Gargi asked such pointed questions of Yajnavalkya that he finally pleaded, "O Gargi, don't ask me anymore; you are asking that which is not to be asked. Stop your questioning or your head will drop down on the floor!"[5] Gargi desisted temporarily, but later returned with new courage, saying "O Yajnavalkya, as the son of a warrior from Kasti or Videha might string his loosened bow, take two pointed arrows in his hand, and rise to do battle, so have I risen to fight you with two supreme questions."[6] Through her questioning, she elicited the understanding of Supreme Reality she sought.

Maitreyi, Yajnavalkya's first wife, had a spiritual yearning comparable to Gargi's. When her husband came to the decision to go away to the forest as a renunciant, leaving his worldly wealth to his two wives, Maitreyi pressed him: "If the whole earth and its treasure were mine, could I attain immortality through them?" Yajnavalkya answered, "No." Maitreyi then asked, "What would I do with that which cannot take me beyond death? Tell me what you know of beyond death."[7] Because of her questioning, she received from him the highest teaching on the nature of the Self.

Women's increasing religious disenfranchisement, along with the disenfranchisement of the lower castes, may be understood as one of the factors that supported the development of heretical sects, the two most important of which were the Jains and the Buddhists. Characteristic of both of these emerging religious sects was a radical democratic spirit. Mahavira (538-c.468 B.C.E.), the reputed founder of Jainism, was an older contemporary of Gautama. But Jain origins reach back some two hundred fifty years earlier, to a sage named

Parsavantha, and thus it was the Jains who first offered an alternative to brahmanic exclusivism. Parsavantha affirmed that a woman was capable of attaining the highest religious goal as a woman; that is to say, she did not need to be reborn as a man. Furthermore, he allowed women the same religious opportunities as men—both could be *sadvis*, "ascetics," or lay followers, and women, like men, could be teachers and preachers. Not only did Jain women enjoy equal rights and privileges with men in the religious sphere, they were also able to take part in political and administrative activities. Moreover, they could appear in public without restriction and all castes could join.

In the generation before Parsavantha, some two thousand women ascetics were said to have realized the highest religious goal in Jainism. Under Parsavantha one generation later, twenty thousand attained this goal (in contrast with one thousand male ascetics). Under Mahavira, we do not have figures of those who became *arahants*, holy ones, but we have a record of the relative number of female and male ascetics and lay followers. There were 36,000 female ascetics and 14,000 male ascetics, 318,000 laywomen and 159,000 laymen.[8] These figures are astonishing in the overwhelming proportion of women represented. They may suggest social unrest; they most definitely suggest brahmanic orthodoxy's inability to accommodate women's religious yearning during this period.

Mahavira organized four distinct communities: female ascetics, male ascetics, laywomen, and laymen. This model of a four-fold community of disciples may have been copied by the Buddha, as we see the same division in early Buddhism. The Jains broke into two main factions. The *Svetambaras* (lit. "white-clad") differed from the *Digambaras* (lit. "sky-clad") on several points, including the roles and capabilities of women. The aphorism *"asti strinirvanam pumvata"* ("like men, women have the right to attain perfection or perfect liberation of the highest order") harks back to Parsavantha. In contrast, though the Digambara sect encouraged women to take up the religious life and practice severe austerities, they did not believe a woman could attain complete emancipation until she was reborn as a man. Further, the Digambaras maintained that nudity was essential for perfection, whereas the Svetambaras believed no harm could come to a person who wore white. As it was considered indecent for a woman in that society to appear naked, she was incapable of attaining complete perfection according to the Digambaras.

Jain women renunciants, like their male counterparts, never established communities in fixed locations. Rather, they followed the ideal of Mahavira, who was said not to have lived more than one day in the same village. Perhaps on account of this ascetic and homeless life, Jain women renunciants did not produce any literature comparable to the *Therigatha*. But we do get confirmation from the *Therigatha* of the existence of Jain women teachers, because we have examples like Bhadda Kundalakesa and Nandutara, Buddhist converts from Jainism, who, prior to their conversion, had wandered and taught widely as Jains.

It is rare to come across actual historical wise women or teachers who predate the *Therigatha*. In the *Jain Canon* we meet (by name only) Jayanti, a queen of Kosambi, who met with Mahavira in order to discuss abstruse points of metaphysics and religion, and who, because of some experience of suffering, decided to become a Jain nun. Also by name we know of Ajja Chandana, Mahavira's first female disciple and the leader of the Jain nuns.

It is only when we come to the Buddhists that we begin to meet by name a number of *acariya*, "women teachers." A special subcategory of *acariya* were the *upajjha*, the women who were actual preceptors, who were spiritual masters and teachers. The development of women teachers may be a by-product of the strict separation of nuns from monks on account of their mutual commitment to celibacy. While the transmission of the teaching was for the most part in the hands of the monks, the rule did allow nuns to give instruction to other nuns. Those women with the most seniority increasingly assumed responsibility for both teaching and running the affairs of their sangha. Examples of such nuns, in addition to Pajapati and Patacara, would be Dhammadinna, renowned as the greatest woman preacher; Sukka, her disciple and heir; Khema; Uppalavanna; Bhadda Kapilani; and others. The stories and poems of three of these women, Dhammadinna, Khema and Uppalavanna are included in this chapter.

DHAMMADINNA

The Buddha considered Dhammadinna to be the foremost among the nuns in the gift of preaching. This skill was held in great esteem, as it directly followed the example of the Buddha, who chose to preach to others rather than remain aloof, enjoying his enlightenment alone.

As a laywoman, Dhammadinna had been the wife of Visakha, an eminent man of Rajagaha. One day, her husband returned home, having heard a sermon of a new religious teacher named Gautama. Normally, when Visakha returned, he would smile if he saw her standing in the window, but on this day he passed without looking. When he entered the door, Dhammadinna held out her hand and welcomed him, but Visakha did not respond. "He must be angry about something," thought Dhammadinna. "I will find out when we sit down to eat." At the meal, when Dhammadinna served the usual boiled rice, it was customary for Visakha to invite her to join him, but instead he ate in silence, not uttering a word.

After the meal, Visakha called Dhammadinna to his side and said that upon hearing this teacher speak, he had experienced a realization, and he was thinking about becoming a monk. Henceforth he would not touch a woman. If he renounced the world, all the wealth of the house would be hers. She could remain here or return to her family. What would she do?

"I wish," replied Dhammadinna after a moment of reflection, "to renounce the world also."

Respecting her intention, Visakha sent her to the community of nuns in a golden palanquin. Resolving to take up her new life in earnest, Dhammadinna retreated to the country, and practiced intensively until she achieved the highest insight. Sometime afterwards, she returned to Rajagaha and revisited her former husband. Visakha, it turned out, had decided not to become a monk. Still, his curiosity was genuine, and he eagerly put questions to her about the Buddha's teaching. These she answered "as easily as one would cut a lotus stalk with a knife."

"What is meditation?" he asked. "What are its outward signs? What is necessary in order to meditate? How do you cultivate it?"

Dhammadinna answered, "Meditation is the focusing of the heart.

Its outward signs are the presence of four kinds of attention. Four kinds of right effort are needed. The way to cultivate it is to practice."[9]

Visakha asked innumerable questions, all of which Dhammadinna answered lucidly. Finally, he asked about nirvana. Dhammadinna said:

> "You will never get to the end of you questionings. For in nirvana the higher life merges to find its goal and its consumation."[10]
>
> And she told him that if he wanted to ask further, he should seek out Gautama. This he did, and, when he related the content of his exchange, the Buddha praised Dhammadinna saying, "Dhammadinna possesses learning and great wisdom. Had you asked me, I would have answered exactly as she did. Her answer was correct and you should treasure it accordingly."[11]

By virtue of having won his complete approval, Dhammadinna's response was declared *buddhavacana*, "the word of the Buddha." As such it is preserved as a discrete scriptural section of the *Majjhima Nikaya*.[12] This is a rare example of *buddhavacana* uttered by a woman disciple. It indicates an equivalence between the Buddha's wisdom and her own.

Dhammadinna's poem is the other example we have of her teaching. In it, she repeats the Buddha's words—an interesting phenomenon considering that the Buddha had declared her words equal to his own. The original of Dhammadinna's poem occurs in the *Dhammapada*, a division of the Pali Canon attributed to the Buddha. In Dhammadinna's version, the masculine nominative forms in Pali are changed to feminine ones. The poem, due to these changes, is thus directed to a woman or women.[13]

As the concept of individual ownership of verses did not exist, we should not consider Dhammadinna's borrowing an instance of plagiarism. To imitate, not only in one's words but in one's actions, as a step towards making the enlightened consciousness one's own, was highly revered.

Eager for the end of suffering,
full of awareness,
that's the way.

When one's heart is not
attached to pleasure, we say,
"That woman has entered the stream."[14]

KHEMA

Khema was one of the two women responsible for running the first community of nuns. She was considered to possess the greatest insight, and in several places in the *Pali Canon* she is called the most exemplary nun.

Khema came from a ruling family in Sagala. She was very beautiful; her skin was said to be the color of pure gold. As a grown woman, she became the chief consort of King Bimbisara. "Chief consort" seems to mean that she was his favorite lover. In this capacity she apparently filled a different niche from Mallika, Bimbisara's chief wife, his other wives Ubirri, Soma, Sakula, Vasabhakhattiya, or his other lovers, female servants, or slaves.

On account of her high status as the King's chief consort and especially on account of her beauty, Khema was very conceited. Though the Buddha paid visits to the royal court, he reputedly spoke ill of beauty and pleasure, and Khema decided she had no interest in hearing him preach. But court poets composed songs on the loveliness of the Veluvana hermitage where the Buddha was staying and, curious to see it, Khema arranged a visit. Indeed the woods and gardens were exquisite. But when she was led before the Buddha, he made an image appear before her of a goddess far more beautiful than she, and showed that woman passing from youth to middle age and finally to old age, with her broken teeth, gray hair, and wrinkled skin. "Will it not be the same for me?" thought Khema. The vision deeply impressed on her the truth of impermanence. Then the Buddha, who knew her thoughts, said that people devoted to physical beauty were bound to the world, while those who renounced the world were free. When he had finished speaking, Khema was enlightened. Hers was a rare instance of enlightenment attained by a laywoman. After this, she left King Bimbisara and became a nun.

A further story about Khema tells of a visit paid to her by the other great king of this period, King Pasenadi of Kosala. More religiously earnest than Bimbisara, Pasenadi came to the nun Khema with his own unanswered question—did a buddha exist after death or not? Though the content of the exchange is not preserved, we know that Khema explained the matter to him fully. She probably made reference to the "indeterminable problems in Buddhism" (*avyakatas*) which the Buddha was said to have left unanswered because he believed they had no bearing on the highest truth. Ten such problems were enumerated, four of which dealt with the question of whether a buddha exists after death or not. Though Khema's teaching to King Pasenadi on this subject was not raised to the status of *buddhavacana*, Khema's teaching was said to have left such an impression on Pasenadi that he later related the incident to the Buddha. That a king should sit at the feet of a woman, in a society where nuns were not permitted to teach monks, shows the high esteem in which Khema was held. That Dhammadinna also taught a man (albeit her former husband) seems to indicate that she too commanded much respect as a teacher.

Khema's poem, full as it is of body-loathing imagery, is not one which is easy to appreciate today, yet it is entirely consistent with Khema's faith. In the first stanza, Mara, the embodiment of evil and death, takes the form of a young man and tries to seduce her. This temptation of Khema by Mara in this fashion parallels Mara's temptation of the Buddha in the form of Mara's three beautiful daughters. The poem shows us that the mature woman, Khema, is no longer conceited. She loathes her body and hasn't the slightest interest in sexual involvement. She sees those who do as fools, seeking satisfaction outside themselves in sensuality or in the worship of material things. As for Khema, she honors the Buddha. Practicing his teaching, she is herself enlightened.

[Mara:]

>Come on, Khema!
>Both of us are young
>and you are beautiful.

Let's enjoy each other!
It will be like the music of a symphony.

[Khema:]

I'm disgusted by this body.
It's foul and diseased.
It torments me.
Your desire for sex
means nothing to me.

Pleasures of the senses are
swords and stakes.
The elements of mind and body
are a chopping block for them.
What you call
delight
is not delight for me.

Everywhere the love of pleasure
is destroyed,
the great dark
is torn apart,
and Death,
you too are destroyed.
Fools,
who don't know things
as they really are,
revere the mansions of the moon
and tend the fire in the wood
thinking this is purity.

But for myself,
I honor the Enlightened One
the best of all
and, practicing his teaching,
am completely freed from suffering.

UPPALAVANNA

While Khema was considered the woman of greatest insight, Uppalavanna was the woman most gifted in magical powers. Together they shared the leadership of the nun's sangha. Uppalavanna was further distinguished, like Pajapati, Patacara, Dhammadinna, Thullananda, and probably Khema, in being able to confer ordination.

Uppalavanna was born in Savatthi, a daughter of a financier, and, like Sundari-Nanda and Khema, was renowned for her beauty. So many men from all over India wanted to marry her that her rich father did not know what to do. Perhaps he secretly longed for the freedom from secular concerns that a renunciant's life offered; perhaps he feared the political rivalry or even battles that might result from the wrong choice of a son-in-law. The story says that he did not wish to offend anyone and so suggested to Uppalavanna that she leave the world. "Dear one," he asked, "are you able to leave the world?" For her part, because of her own religious leanings, "his words fell as if oil a hundred times refined had annointed her head."[15]

One of the many men who desired Uppalavanna was a cousin of hers, a young man named Ananda. (He should not be confused with Gautama's cousin and attendant by the same name.) Ananda did not want Uppalavanna to renounce the world. Sometime during the first years following Uppalavanna's ordination, Ananda found out that she lived alone in a hut in Andhavana. One day while she was out, Ananda hid himself under her bed. When she returned and lay down on her bed, he suddenly jumped out and raped her. Though his punishment was to be eaten by the fires of Avici, the most frightful of the many Buddhist hells, the punishment that Buddhist nuns incurred was more enduring. Because of this incident, Buddhist nuns from that time to the present have been forbidden to go out alone or to live as hermits in the woods.[16] This was a great penalty indeed, considering that the solitary renunciant is an esteemed vocation and role.

Subsequently, Uppalavanna took up residence within the community of nuns. On a certain day, when it was her turn to perform certain ceremonies in the *uposatha* hall, she swept the room and lit a lamp, and then, using the lamp's flame as the object of her meditation, she achieved deep concentration and attained enlightenment. Eventually, she acquired a number of supernatural powers, including the ability to adopt another form (*vikubbana*).

As a mature woman, Uppalavanna was permitted to ordain other women. Originally, this privilege was solely the Buddha's. Later, senior monks and eventually senior nuns gained this status as well. The story still exists of Uppalavanna's ordination of a remarkable laywoman, Anoja.

Anoja was the wife of King Mahakappina, of equal rank to him in birth. When Mahakappina made the decision to become a Buddhist renunciant, Anoja and her companions sought to do the same, saying, "The Buddha could not have arisen only for the benefit of men, but for women as well." Then Anoja and the women went to listen to the Buddha preach. Hearing his words, they all became "stream-enterers," the first of four levels of Buddhist realization. Her husband, Mahakappina, was present at this gathering, but the Buddha, using his own magic powers, made the king invisible. Then he asked Anoja, "Would you rather seek the king or seek yourself?"

Without hesitation she replied, "Myself," thereby demonstrating her insight as well as her sincerity. Afterwards, she went to the community of nuns and was ordained by Uppalavanna.[17]

In the text of the *Therigatha*, Uppalavanna's verses all run together. The Commentary breaks them into four separate poems and, for the sake of clarity, that format has been followed here. Caroline Rhys Davids speaks of Uppalavanna's verses as: "a collection of detached *gathas* where no organic melding has been attempted." She goes on to explain that Uppalavanna's name occurs more frequently in various Pali texts than that of any other woman's name. Along with the *theri* Khema, Uppalavanna is held up by the Buddha as the model of what a woman in holy orders should be.[18] But in the *Vinaya*, a *bhikkhuni* named Uppalavanna is cited twice as a woman attractive to the opposite sex and once as a student of weak memory. Another name too, that of Ummadanti ("enchantress") is mixed up with hers. Rhys Davids concludes that, "The great *theri* of supernormal power is as difficult to identify as our own St. George and it is not strange that her *gatha* should be composite."[19]

In Uppalavanna's first poem, it is unclear whether she is recounting her own story or telling a folk story.[20] In either case, it is a rather bizarre tale, reminiscent of the Greek tragedy, *Oedipus Rex.* The following synopsis will provide the reader with the details omitted from the poem. For the sake of clarity, the mother has been given the name Mata (Pali for "mother") to distinguish her from her unnamed daughter. Mata's son is referred to by his Buddhist name, Gangatiriya.

Mata was a merchant's wife in Savatthi. While her husband was away on a prolonged business trip in Rajagaha, Mata found out she was pregnant. The mother-in-law, accusing her of infidelity, turned Mata out of the house. Alone, heading along the highways in search of her husband, Mata felt the onset of labor, and in a wayside hut delivered a son, Gangatiriya. Next an evil merchant came along, stole her son from her, and raised the child as his own. Later, the distraught mother was taken in by a robber chief. By this man, Mata bore a daughter. Then one day, by mistake, Mata injured the child, and fearing the robber's wrath, she fled from him, leaving her daughter behind. Many years later, Gangatiriya independently married both Mata and her daughter. One day, to her horror, Mata discovered the scar on her young co-wife's head, which identified the woman as her own daughter. This poem is spoken by that unnamed daughter, who may or may not be Uppalavanna.[21]

The second poem is simply a stock poem which we will encounter again in several later chapters. It is meant to declare the speaker's complete enlightenment.

The third poem, like the first, has a story behind it. As already mentioned, Uppalavanna had magical powers. One day when the Buddha was about to perform miracles, Uppalavanna offered to perform some of her own. Her intention was to assume the form of a *cakkavatti*, a "great ruler," followed by a retinue extending 30,000 leagues. According to the story, the Buddha would not consent to the performance of these miracles. According to the poem, the miracles seem to have taken place anyway.

Finally, the fourth poem, a dialogue between Mara and Uppalavanna, is spoken in a sal tree grove. Its final three stanzas are common stock passages.

I

My mother and I found out
we were wives of the same man.
I was horrified,
my hair stood on end,
and suddenly the pleasures of the senses
were vile and stinking to me.
I loathed them and all the troubles they
caused
where mother and daughter
were wives together.

Then pleasure
was danger,
and renunciation
was solid ground,

so at Rajagaha,
I left home to be homeless.

II

Now I have entered
the six realms of sacred knowledge:
I know that I have lived before,
the eye of heaven has grown clear,
my hearing is pure,
and I know the minds of others.
I have great magic powers
and have annihilated all
the obsessions of the mind;
the Buddha's teaching has been done.

III

To show my power
I made a four-horse chariot;
then I paid homage at the feet
of the Buddha,

the refuge of the world,
and stood beside him.

IV

[Mara:]

You're just a child
standing alone
at the foot of the flowering tree.
You don't even have a companion—
aren't you afraid of bad men?

[Uppalavanna:]

Mara, if 100,000 men as bad as you
came all together,
I wouldn't move a hair.
What can you do on your own?

[Mara:]

I'll vanish!
I'll enter your belly!
I'll stand between your eyebrows
and you won't be able to see me!

[Uppalavanna:]

My mind is my own.
I have walked the roads to power
and have discovered the great knowledges.
The Buddha's teaching has been done.

Pleasures of the senses
are swords and stakes,
the elements of mind and body
are a chopping block for them.

What you call
delight
is not delight for me.

Everywhere the love of pleasure
is destroyed
the great dark
is torn apart
and Death,
you too are destroyed.

[1] J.P. Mallory. *In Search of the Indo-Europeans: Language, Archeology and Myth*. (London: Thames and Hudson, 1989), p. 45.

[2] Monica Sjoo and Barbara Mor. *The Great Cosmic Mother*. (San Francisco: Harper and Row, 1987), p. 219.

[3] Shakuntala Rao Shastri. *Women in the Vedic Age*. (Bombay: Baratiya Vidya Bhavan, 1969), pp. 117-122.

[4] *Ibid.*, p. 23-29.

[5] *Ibid.*, p. 91.

[6] Professor Indra. *Status of Women in Ancient India*. (Banaras: Motilal Banarsidass, 1955), p. 138.

[7] Shakuntala Rao Shastri. *Op. Cit.*, p. 94-95.

[8] Sri Sankar Sen Gupta. *Women in Indian Folklore*. (Calcutta: Indian Publications, 1969), p. 35.

[9] Lord Chalmers. *Further Dialogues of the Buddha*. Vol. I. (London: Oxford University Press, 1926), p. 215. This passage is my adaptation of Chalmers' translation.

[10] *Ibid.*, p. 218.

[11] *Ibid.*, p. 218.

[12] *Culla Vedalla Sutta. Op. Cit.*, pp. 213-218.

[13] *Dhammapada*. Chapter 16, verse 218. For a discussion of the masculine and feminine forms in the *Dhammapada* and *Therigatha* versions, see K.R. Norman. *The Elders Verses II*. (London: Published for the Pali Text Society by Luzac and Co., 1971), p. 58.

[14] *Uddhan-sota*, lit. "stream-enterer." A stream-enterer is a person who has destroyed the first five of the ten fetters, the destruction of all ten of which constitutes nirvana in this lifetime.

[15] Caroline Rhys Davids. *Psalms of the Sisters*. (London: Henry Frowde, Oxford University Press Warehouse, 1909), p. 112.

[16] Max Müller, ed. *Vinaya Texts*. Part III. Translated by T.W. Rhys Davids and Hermann Oldenberg. *The Sacred Books of the East*. Vol. XX. (Oxford: Clarendon Press, 1885), pp. 362-363.

[17] George Malalasekera. *Dictionary of Pali Proper Names*. (London: Luzac and Co., 1960), p. 96.

[18] *Samyutta Nikaya* ii 236.

[19] Caroline Rhys Davids. *Op. Cit.*, pp. xx-xxi.

[20] See I.B. Horner. *Women Under Primitive Buddhism*. (London: George Routledge and Sons, Ltd., 1930. Rep. by Asia Books Corp.), p. 37, and Caroline Rhys Davids. *Op. Cit.*, p. 115, for two different points of view on Uppalavanna's first poem.

[21] Caroline Rhys Davids. *Op Cit.*, p. 115.

CHAPTER FIVE

Mothers

This chapter includes stories and poems of five women who were mothers. Though this chapter is about motherhood, all of the stories and poems share another theme—grief. The mothers of this chapter were motivated to become Buddhist nuns by grief over the death of their children, perhaps the most painful and incomprehensible loss. Throughout history child mortality has been commonplace, and the mother's loss of her child is a recurring literary and religious theme. It is central to the myth of Demeter and Persephone, which provided the mythological and theological foundation for the religious rites of the Eleusinian Mysteries.

The story goes that Demeter, the Greek goddess of the fruits of harvest, dearly loved her daughter. One day when Persephone was out in the fields picking flowers with her friends, the girl noticed a narcissus of striking beauty. When she bent to pick it, the earth gaped open and Hades, Lord of Death, appeared. He seized her and dragged her down to his underworld kingdom. Hearing her daughter's cry, Demeter ranged the world, searching, but in vain. Finally, after nine days, she learned that Zeus had awarded Persephone to his brother, Hades; and the revelation overwhelmed her. She went mad; she was completely willing to let the world die because of her grief:

> And she made this
> the most terrible year
> on this earth
> that feeds so many,
> and the most cruel.
> The earth
> did not take seed
> that year...
>
> And in fact
> she could have wiped out
> the whole race

of talking men
with a painful famine
and deprived
those who live on Olympus
of the glorious honor
of offerings and sacrifice.[1]

Better known still is the story of Mary's grief over the crucifixion of Jesus, expressed in one stark line from John 19: 25-26.

Near the cross of Jesus stood his mother.[2]

Apart from this one line, the Gospels remained silent on Mary's grief. But the theme proved sufficiently powerful to be taken up by the Catholic Church in the Middle Ages and greatly explored in both art and literature.

Likewise, the mother's loss of a child in the Buddhist era had its own unique meaning. To understand that meaning, we must first understand the special role of mother in Indian society. Sources for the veneration of the mother in India are found in prehistoric times. In the Neolithic and Paleolithic eras, the mother was the focal point of the clan, responsible for the bearing, rearing, and teaching of the young. She was the symbol of life, generation, and fertility.

In contrast, Vedic society was a patriarchal one. Aditi was the only Vedic goddess of any stature, and by this time women's status was rather low. The Brahmanic conception of dharma viewed society as an organism in which everyone and everything had a place. This "place" was simultaneously a "nature" and a "role." A woman's dharma was to become a mother and bear sons, ten sons being the ideal number. It was her natural calling and the means to channel her strong generative drive. Her dharma also implied that she be subordinate to men—to her father in childhood, to her husband in maturity, to her sons in old age. By accepting her place and fulfilling her dharma as a mother, a woman was deserving of honor. Out of place, she was suspect. Brahmanic society was uncomfortable with women who failed to fulfill this ideal role, uncomfortable with female ascetics, and with single, childless, or widowed women.[3]

The brahman Vaisista shows the high regard the woman could achieve as a mother:

> The teacher is ten times more venerable than the assistant teacher, the father a hundred times more than the teacher, and the mother a thousand times more than the father.[4]

This veneration of the mother may also account for the fact that the mother's name is commonly mentioned first in passages from early Sanskrit and Pali texts when the names of both parents are listed.[5]

The cult of the mother was ancient by the sixth century B.C.E. So sound and timeless a feature of early Indian society was the cult, that it was not particularly affected by Buddhism. I.B. Horner tells us that, "Buddhism took up the cult as it found it and did nothing to alter it."[6] Kisagotami's story in this chapter is evidence for Horner's viewpoint. Kisagotami was from a poor family and, as a young bride, was mistreated by her in-laws. But when she bore her first child, a son, she gained authority and respect within the household. Motherhood remained the most honored phase of a woman's life in early Buddhist culture as well.

So important was it for a woman to give birth to a child that it was customary to name a woman after her child. Padumavati, the courtesan of Ujjeni, was called "Abhayamata" (Abhaya being her child's name, *mata* being the word for mother). Similarly Vaddhamata and, from this chapter, Sumangalamata, were both named after their children. Though these are examples from the sixth century B.C.E., this custom continues in India even today. A similar custom popular during the early Buddhist period was for men to call themselves by their mother's name. Sariputta, the famed disciple of the Buddha, was the son of the brahman woman Sari. Mantaniputta was the son of the woman Mantani.

The mother was characterized by archetypal traits such as devotion, compassion, and self-sacrifice. Motherly love was a prototype for all love and could be an appropriate theme for meditation:

> If we contemplate on our own mother's kindness towards us, our fondness for her will grow. Before our birth we were pro-

tected and preciously carried in her womb. We were in a state of total helplessness and complete dependence. Our presence there was not only a great physical burden to her, but was also a responsibility curtailing her freedom of action. When eating, walking, sitting or sleeping, she was constrained to be mindful of our presence and welfare. This she did joyfully. At birth, we gave great suffering to our mother, yet she forgot this at once and rejoiced as though she had found a precious gem. We had no control over our physical functions, yet she felt no revulsion towards our vomit or excretions and cared for us gently. When she looked at us and spoke our name she did so in a special way. Her tenderness was not in response to some kindness we had shown her, but was the result of her enormous compassion. Without her constant attention we would not be alive now. She did not do so in hope of repayment nor because she was compelled to do so. When it was a question of her personal benefit and ours, she sacrificed her own benefit and well-being.[7]

Not only is this the instruction in a particular Buddhist meditation, it is the statement of the ideal of selfless devotion and compassion which the mother is meant to incarnate. We could also read it as a creed for the cult of the mother.

While Buddhism inherited the cult of the mother and left it unchanged, the Buddha used the metaphors of motherly love as teaching devices to suit different purposes. In a famous Pali verse attributed to the Buddha and recited down the centuries in Theravadin Buddhist countries, the disciple is exhorted as follows:

> Just as the mother at the risk of life,
> loves and protects her son, her only son.
> So let him [the monk] cultivate this
> boundless love
> to all that live in the whole universe...
> When he lives with perfect insight won,
> he surely comes no more to any womb.[8]

This verse is fascinating in that it both uses and undercuts the ideal of motherly love. The monk seeks to cultivate a love as strong as the mother's, but then to extend it beyond the limits of that one relationship. By cultivating universal love, he will achieve perfect insight and will come no more to any womb. Here is the irony, which, though not explicitly stated, seems to be the philosophical underpinning. Through this cultivated power and insight, the monk will cut off future rebirths and thereby transcend the woman's power to give birth.

Clearly, such an interpretation does not hold birth or women's power to give birth in high esteem. Under the Buddhist system, a woman, regardless of her role, was considered to belong to an intermediate plane between animals and men. To be born into a woman's body was considered a cause for special suffering on account of menstruation, childbirth, and menopause. Although a woman could achieve the highest goal of *nirvana*, still, it was considered the greatest merit for a woman to be reborn as a man. The mother's tie to her child was a common metaphor for attachment to the world of *samsara*. That tie is the polar opposite of the monk's detachment.

As we pursue this irony, we detect other contradictions. One would think that because a key Buddhist goal was to cut off rebirth, and because the surest way to achieve that goal was through renunciation, then the women who didn't conceive might be applauded. Nevertheless, among the Buddhists, childlessness was still considered a great misfortune. This may hark back to the Brahmanic expectation that a mother bear sons. It may go back still further to a prehistoric valuation of fertility. It may be the result simply of the natural human joy and appreciation of new life. Whatever the reason, a barren woman was dealt a terrible blow. She suffered the emotional burden of not achieving the respect and honor she could expect to gain as a mother. Also, she was ruined on a more everyday level because her husband could bring a new wife into the household. Not only did she not gain honor and authority; henceforth she was seen as a burden on the household.

A contemporary story points not only to the tragedy of a barren Indian woman's situation but to the depth, timelessness, and archetypal nature of the themes with which we are dealing. The following story is so like the ones in this chapter that it could have been told in 500 B.C.E., as much as in 1980 when it was told. This story was told to me by a Buddhist woman teacher, Krishna Barua, who had been a disciple under Munindra.

Krishna was Bengali and one of her closest disciples was also from Bengal. That disciple had once been an intelligent and politically active woman who, when she came of age, was married by the arrangement of her parents. She moved to an extended family of in-laws, all of whom were strangers to her. Her husband was the eldest son. By him she was unable to conceive. The burden of her situation weighed more and more heavily on her, until finally, when the next eldest son and his new wife gave birth to a child, something snapped.

When she was brought to Krishna, the woman was insane. She had been treated in a number of asylums, and she was so broken by these experiences that she could not even walk, and had to be carried in by her husband and brother-in-law. Under ordinary circumstances, those with mental health problems were not accepted as disciples, but Krishna was moved by this poor woman's condition, and she agreed to accept her.

Krishna served her tea and taught her a simple meditation. Then she showed the woman a place to practice the instruction. After ten minutes, Krishna noticed a smile come over the woman's face. Next, Krishna taught her the technique of walking meditation, and almost immediately the woman regained her ability to walk. Later, when Krishna left India to teach in the United States, she parted from a sane and devoted disciple and friend.

This story of a contemporary woman gone mad because she could not conceive relates directly to the women of this chapter. Of the eighteen married women whose verses appear in the *Therigatha*, six had experienced the loss of a child. In a culture that taught women to lose and find themselves in mothering, infertility or the death of a child was a cause for terrible despair. All the women in this chapter have known that despair:

KISAGOTAMI

Miserable woman,
this pain can't be measured.
Your tears have been falling
for thousands of lives.

VASETTHI

Grief-stricken for my son
totally mad, out of my senses...

On the other side of that despair, some women found unshakable equanamity. While the women in this chapter could be said to have gained that peace "through the means of motherhood," it should be understood that almost no Buddhist women arahants were actively engaged in mothering. From the evidence of the stories and poems, the two roles seem to have been mutually exclusive. The nun's child or children had grown up, been entrusted to the care of a family member, or died. The case of a woman who entered the nuns' sangha ignorant of the fact she was pregnant and whose child was raised by the nuns' sangha is a notable exception.[9] Although the Buddhist nuns did not live out the Indian ideal of motherhood, there was a treasure at the end of their path: freedom. As one nun eloquently summed up:

Now, though I am the same woman,
I know freedom from birth and death
and do not grieve or weep.

UBBIRI

The poems of the *Therigatha*, as testimonies of women's achievement of arahantship, present us with a number of unique examples of great women teachers, wanderers, and nuns. The story of Ubbiri is unique in the *Therigatha* in that she attains arahantship as a laywoman. Though her subsequent entry into the ordained sangha might be assumed, it is not mentioned.

Ubbiri came from an eminent family of Savatthi. She was a beautiful child, and when she had grown, was brought to the court of Pasenadi, the King of Kosala. By him, she bore a daughter and named her Jiva, which means "alive." But shortly thereafter, Jiva died, and day after day the mother went mourning to the cremation grounds. On one of these days, a crowd had gathered to listen to Siddhartha Gautama as he was passing through town. Ubbiri paused momentarily at the edge of the crowd, but soon left and stood by the Achiravati River, weeping.

Seeing her, Gautama approached and asked why she wept.

"My daughter is dead! My daughter is dead!" she cried.

"Look!" he said. "Here and here! Eighty-four thousand of your daughters are buried in this place. For which one do you grieve?" And pointing out the places where this one and that one had been laid, he spoke the first stanza of this poem, to which Ubbiri replied with the last two stanzas.

[Buddha:]

> Mother, you cry out "O Jiva" in the woods.
> Come to yourself, Ubbiri.
> Eighty-four thousand daughters
> all with the name "Jiva"
> have burned in the funeral fire.
> For which one do you grieve?

[Ubbiri:]

> I had an arrow hidden in my heart
> and he took it out—
> that grief for my daughter.
>
> The arrow is out,
> The heart healed of hunger.
> I take refuge in the Buddha-sage,
> the Dharma, the Sangha.

PATACARA PANCASATA

We already met the great teacher named Patacara in Chapter Two. Here we meet Patacara Pancasata. Who is she? Caroline Rhys Davids, in translating Pancasata as "five-hundred," figured that here was another poem by a group of women, comparable to the poem "Thirty Nuns under Patacara." K.R. Norman, on the other hand, has suggested that Pancasata may mean "mindful of the five," perhaps referring to the five *skandhas* or the five *nirvanas*, and feels that this was an epithet given to another Patacara, perhaps to distinguish her from her more renowned namesake. According to Dhammapala, the great commentator on the *Therigatha*, the first four stanzas of this poem were originally spoken by Patacara in order to counsel five hundred women before they became nuns. The following six stanzas were uttered after these women had become ordained. Because they had received their admonition from Patacara, the five hundred women were afterwards called "Patacara's Five Hundred."[10]

Here we will follow Caroline Rhys Davids' and Dhammapala's interpretation. The poem is a dialogue between Patacara and a group of her disciples who had been mothers but lost their children. As such, it belongs to a genre of poems called "dialogue poems," in which there is more than one speaker. However, this is not a dialogue between Patacara and five hundred disciples. Rather, as with Mahapajapati's Five Hundred, we can understand five hundred to mean "a great many." But whether five hundred or fifty, the fact that we are dealing with "a great many" lends further support to the supposition that Patacara had a very large following. As she herself had been a mother who had known grief and loss, she was an example to a number of other mothers. We can assume that women who shared similar losses would have been drawn to Patacara for comfort, support, and direction in building a new and meaningful life.

Pancasata Patacara's poem is repetitive and suffers in the transposition from an oral utterance, in which repetition can serve to heighten appreciation, to a literary poem on the page. As a written poem, it needs editing and cutting. We should read it with sensitivity to this fact.

> You cry out, "My son!"
> You don't know his coming and going.
> You grieve,
> but who knows where he came from?
>
> Everything alive is like this,
> You wouldn't grieve
> about his coming and going
> if you understood.

He came unasked.
He left,
and there is nothing you could do;
he must have come from somewhere
and he lived just a few days.

He came by one road,
he is leaving by another;
he has gone from the human world,
and his journey will go on.
He came. He went.
What is there to cry about?

She pulled out the arrow
hidden in my heart,
that grief for my son.
I was helpless with grief.
She has thrust it away.
Today it is gone;
I am free and want nothing.

I take refuge in the Buddha-sage,
the Dharma, and the Sangha.

VASETTHI

Having read the stories and poems of Ubbiri, Pancasata Patacara, and Kisagotami, the story and poem of Vasetthi may seem more of a type-story than an individual one. Nevertheless, it speaks of the very real condition of a woman's life in that period, and indeed throughout much of human history—a mother's grief and even madness over the loss of her child.

Vasetthi was born in Vesali and was happily married to a man by whom she bore a son. When her child died, she went mad and ran away from home. There were no institutions for a person in such extreme grief, and Vasetthi roamed from place to place like an unwanted animal. Eventually, she came to Mithila, encountered the Buddha, and regained her sanity. Then Vasetthi joined the nuns' sangha and later became an *arahant*.

Grief-stricken for my son,
mad-minded, out of my senses,
I was naked with wild hair
and I wandered anywhere.

I lived on trash heaps,
in a graveyard,
and by the highways.
Three years' wandering,
starved and thirsty.

Then in the city of Mithila
I saw the one who tames
what is untamed
and goes his way in happiness,
enlightened, unafraid.

I came to my senses,
paid homage,
and sat down.

Out of compassion,
Gautama taught me the way.
When I heard his words
I set out into homelessness.
By putting his teachings into practice,
I realized great joy.

My grief is cut out,
finished, ended,
for I have understood the ground
from which all grief comes.

KISAGOTAMI

Kisagotami came from a poor family of Savatthi. She was called "Kisa," meaning thin; her thinness was probably due to the poverty in which she had grown up. Gotami was her family name. Her mother's brother was Suddhodana, the father of the Buddha; Siddhartha Gautama was her cousin.

Kisagotami had one noteworthy encounter with her cousin when both were still living with their families in Kapilavatthu. It occurred on the day Siddhartha's son, Rahula, was born. The new father, having learned of the birth, was en route home. Noticing Siddhartha's radiance, Kisagotami commented that the mother and father of such a son as Siddhartha, and the wife of such a husband, must surely be happy.

Sometime later, Kisagotami was married to a banker's son of considerable wealth. As a young wife, Kisagotami was mistreated by her in-laws, as new brides who moved into their husbands' home sometimes were. When she gave birth to a son, she finally received an honorable place among her husband's relatives. But her child died while still a toddler, and Kisagotami, who had never seen death before, went mad.

In her state of insanity, Kisagotami took up the dead child and carried him on her hip from house to house, begging for medicine. One kind old man directed her to the Buddha.

The Buddha said, "Go and bring a white mustard seed from a house where no one has died." Hearing his words, she immediately rushed off in the innocent faith that if she brought a white mustard seed to this enlightened sage, it would be the medicine that could miraculously bring her child back to life.

Kisagotami went from house to house, at each house asking, and at each house learning that there too, someone had died. The truth struck home. Her sanity returned.

"Little son," she said. "I thought that death had happened to you alone; but it is not to you alone. It is common to all people."

Then, still holding the body of her child in her arms, she carried him gently to the forest and left him there.

Returning to the Buddha, Kisagotami requested and received ordination. She became preeminent among the nuns for her asceticism. With this austerity as her trademark, she ultimately gained the peace of *nirvana*.

Kisagotami's poem is another which is not easily accessible as a literary work in translation, yet it is an important poem deserving of our effort. We need to understand the poem as a composite work, the product of an oral tradition, not a one-time utterance by one person. We need to identify the various possible units in the poem to recognize the poem not as the utterance of one but several voices.

In the previous chapter, we saw the example of Uppalavanna's poem, a collection of detached stanzas where no organic melding had taken place. Following the *Therigatha* Commentary, we presented Uppalavanna's poem as four individual units. Kisagotami's poem is a similar collection of detached stanzas where partial, though unsuccessful, melding seems to have been attempted. Woven into the center of Kisagotami's poem is the tragedy of Patacara's life. Caroline Rhys Davids comments, "It is very probable from inspection of the poem (and chronicle), that of the two poems attributed to Patacara, one recounting her sufferings, given in the *Apadana* and quoted in the Commentary, has been lost or merged with that of Kisagotami."[11]

Given this interpolation at the heart of Kisagotami's poem, I have divided the poem into four units and labeled each as to the speaker. The first unit is comprised of stanzas one through three, unified by the common theme of the Buddha's wisdom and teaching. Stanza four, because it relates only loosely with the first unit, is considered a discrete second unit. The only theme common to units one and two, which does not seem sufficient to knit them into one unit, is suffering.

The middle stanzas, five through eight, may be Kisagotami's citation of Patacara's experience for the purpose of giving greater depth to her own expression of suffering. Or, more likely, these stanzas may be misattributed to Kisagotami, and in fact belong as a unit to Patacara. These middle stanzas are presented as a long third unit.

The problem with the last unit—stanzas nine, ten, and eleven— is that the previous unit best fits Patacara's, not Kisagotami's story, and yet Kisagotami has included her name in the final line of stanza eleven. This is the only poem in the *Therigatha* with a signature line.

As we turn now to the poem, bear in mind that all these divisions are tentative. Their purpose is to make the poem more accessible to the English reader, while maintaining the integrity of the original, as it has come down to us.

I

[Kisagotami:]

    The Sage looked at the world
    and said—
    with good friends
    even a fool can be wise.

    Keep good company,
    and wisdom grows.
    Those who keep good company
    can be freed from suffering.

    We have to understand suffering
    the cause of suffering,
    its end,
    and the Eightfold Way—
    these are the Four Noble Truths.

II

[Kisagotami:]

    The Guide of a restless,
    passionate humanity has said—
    to be a woman is to suffer.
    To live with co-wives is suffering.
    Women can give birth
    and, becoming depressed,
    cut their throats.
    Beautiful young women eat poison,
    but both will suffer in hell
    when the mother-murdering fetus
    comes not to life.[12]

III

[Patacara:]

    On a journey, near to childbirth
    I found my husband dead
    and gave birth on the road;
    I hadn't reached my family's home.

I lost both sons
and my husband dead on the road,
then mother, father, brother
burning on one pyre.

[Buddha or an enlightened nun:]
(Miserable woman,
your family is destroyed,
this pain can't be measured,
and your tears have been falling
for thousands of lives.)

[Patacara:]
I have seen the jackals
eating the flesh of my sons
in the cemetery.
My family destroyed,
my husband dead,
despised by everyone,
I found what does not die.

IV

[Kisagotami:]
I have practiced the Great
Eightfold Way
straight to the undying.
I have come to the great peace
I have looked into the mirror
of the Dharma.

The arrow is out.
I have put my burden down.
What had to be done has been done.

Sister Kisagotami
with a free mind
has said this.

KISAGOTAMI

A second story-poem attributed to Kisagotami is included here. It is
not from the *Therigatha*, but from the *Samyutta Nikaya*.[13] We may
presume from the context that it is spoken by Kisagotami in the new
phase of her life as a nun. In it, Kisagotami, in dialogue with Mara,
the incarnation of Death, refers to her dead child, saying, "I don't
grieve. I don't cry. I'm not afraid of you, friend."

The piece, like others from the *Bhikkhuni Samyutta*—the second
collection of nuns' poetry from the *Pali Canon*—mixes prose and
verse. Winternitz comments that "Some of these short ballads about
Mara and the nuns, which are remarkable also for the sake of their
archaic language, are among the most beautiful productions of ancient Indian poetic art."[14]

It is included for this reason, and seems to be an appropriate ending for this chapter because it shows how a woman, overcome by terrible loss, emerges with new spiritual insight.

Thus have I heard. Once when at Savatthi, the Lord
stayed at Anathapindika's Jeta Grove. The nun,
Kisagotami, having dressed, went one morning into
town with her robe and bowl to beg for food. After her
almsround and after she had returned with her
almsfood, she ate, then went into the dark forest to
spend the day there. Arriving in the dark forest, she sat
down at the foot of a tree.

Then Mara, the Evil One, wanting to inspire fear and
terror and to ruin her meditation, went to that same
place. Having gone there, he spoke this verse to her:

[Mara:]

> What's going on?
> You look as if your child has died.
> You sit alone;
> tears streak your face.
> You've come to the woods alone—
> are you looking for a man?

But Kisagotami thought, "Is this a human being or not?
It must be Mara. He has spoken this verse because he
wants to terrify me and ruin my meditation." When she
knew this for certain, that this was none other than the
Evil One, Mara, she addressed him as follows:

[Kisagotami:]

> I have finished with the death of my child,
> and men belong to that past.
> I don't grieve.
> I don't cry.
> I'm not afraid of you, friend.
>
> Everywhere the love of pleasure is destroyed,
> the great dark is torn apart,
> and Death,
> you too are destroyed.

[1] Christine Downing. "Goddess Sent Madness," in *Psychological Perspectives*. (Fall 1981), p. 143.

[2] *The Jerusalem Bible*. (New York: Doubleday and Co., 1966), p. 187.

[3] Nancy A. Falk and Rita Gross, ed. *Unspoken Worlds*. (San Francisco: Harper and Row, 1982), pp. 221-222.

[4] Meena Talim. *Women in Early Buddhist Literature*. (Bombay: University of Bombay, 1972), p. 144.

[5] I.B. Horner. *Women Under Primitive Buddhism*. (London: George Routledge and Sons, Ltd., 1930), p. 5.

[6] *Ibid.*, p. 4.

[7] Ven. Geshe Rabten. *The Preliminary Practices of Tibetan Meditation*. (Burton, Washington: Tusum Ling Publishers, 1974), p. 37.

[8] *Suttanipata* 148. Phra Khantipalo, tr. Version used in sutra service at Wiseman's Ferry, New South Wales, Australia.

[9] Max Müller, ed. *Vinaya Texts*. Part III. *Sacred Books of the East*. Vol. XX. (Oxford: Clarendon Press, 1885 Rep. by Delhi: Motilal Banarsidass, 1969), p. 364.

[10] Richard Pischel, ed. *The Therigatha*. (London: Henry Frowde, Oxford University Press Warehouse, 1883), p. 121.

[11] Caroline Rhys Davids. *Psalms of Sisters*. (London: Henry Frowde, Oxford University Press Warehouse, 1909), p. xxi.

[12] It is ambiguous whether the term *ubho* (lit. "both") in this sentence refers to the two kinds of women who are suffering on account of their suicides, to two co-wives, or to the mother and her unborn child. In this translation, I have retained that ambiguity on the grounds that the original may be suggesting two or possibly even all three interpretations. The Pali is elusive. My own speculation is that the stanza refers to one of several possible situations. The stanza could be an enumeration of a variety of ways women suffer: (1) as a co-wife, (2) giving birth, or (3) on account of abortion. More obliquely, it may refer to a hatred commonly known to exist between a first wife and a rival wife. When the poem tells us that "Women give birth once and cut their throats," it may be implying that a first wife, if she doesn't want to go through the pain of childbirth again or is not sexually desirable to certain men, both literally and figuratively "cuts her throat." She will have a rival, a young beautiful woman who, out of innocence or fear, will accept poison from an elder co-wife. Such young women may suffer abortion, miscarriage, or even death. The Sattaputtakhadaka of *Petavatthu* is my source for this interpretation. There, an elder wife, with the help of a physician, causes an abortion in her pregnant co-wife. This is but one among many examples from the *Petavatthu* of a first wife causing a rival wife to abort or miscarry. It is said that many departed spirits suffer in hell on account of their having committed such crimes. See also Meena Talim. *Op. Cit.*, p. 132.

[13] Caroline Rhys Davids, ed. *Samyutta Nikaya*. Part I. *Bhikkhuni Samyutta*. Text i, 128. (London: Pali Text Society, 1917), p. 162.

[14] Maurice Winternitz. *A History of Indian Literature*. (Calcutta: University of Calcutta, 1933), p. 58.

CHAPTER SIX

Wives

The overwhelming majority of women in sixth century B.C.E. Indian society lived not as single women, nuns, prostitutes or courtesans, but as wives. Perhaps because this was the most common life-path for women, there is a comparatively large amount of information in the Pali Buddhist literature about married women. Much is said about wives in classical Sanskrit literature as well, because Vedic culture favored a married life and only came to value renunciation in the Upanishadic period, roughly contemporary with the early Buddhist period.

When the monk Anuruddha asked the Buddha what qualities enabled a woman to go to heaven (literally, to be in the company of the *devas*), the Buddha replied that if the woman were a wife, she should have these five qualities: (1) She should get up before her husband and go to bed after him. (2) She should honor and respect a person whom her husband honors and respects. (3) She should know in detail about servants in the house, messengers, and menials. She should know the workers appointed to them, know their wages, and look after them when they are sick. (4) She should help her husband in home industries. (5) She should keep watch on the money, grain, silver or gold, which her husband brings home.[1]

Elsewhere, the Buddha claims that the ideal wife should act as a mother, a sister, a friend, or a slave towards her husband.[2] A perfect wife is one of the seven gems possessed by a *cakkavattin* (a "just and faithful Buddhist ruler"). The Buddha describes such a wife to Ananda:

> She is graceful in figure, beautiful in appearance, charming, most fine in complexion, neither very stout nor very slim, neither dark nor very fair, surpassing in human beauty. Her touch is as soft as that of cotton wool. In cold season, her limbs are warm; in heat, her limbs are cool. Her body wears the perfume of sandalwood and from her mouth emanates the perfume of lotus. She rises up before her husband and retires after he retires to rest; pleasant is she in speech, ever on the watch to

hear what she may do in order to please him. Never in thought
is she unfaithful to the king, much less in body. [3]

The Buddhist nun Isadasi, before her renunciation, strove to em-
body these virtues. She expresses her effort in a late poem from
the *Therigatha*. [4]

> In the splendid city of Ujjeni,
> my father was a good merchant.
> I was his only daughter,
> charming and beloved.
>
> Then a rich merchant from Saketa
> sent a man of a noble family
> to ask for me.
> My father gave me to that merchant
> as a daughter-in-law.
>
> Morning and evening
> I bowed to the feet
> of my father-in-law and mother-in-law.
> If I saw my beloved,
> his sisters, his brothers,
> or even his retinue,
> I trembled and gave up my seat.
> I tried to please them
> with every kind of food and drink,
> and gave to all the proper portions.
>
> I rose early and went to my lord's room,
> having already washed my hands and feet,
> and on the threshold I came to him with
> cupped hands.
> Bringing comb, mirror, soap,
> and ornaments as though I were a servant,
> I dressed him and groomed him myself.

I boiled the rice,
I washed the pots,
and looked after him
as a mother would her only son.

And though I was devoted to him,
a humble and affectionate servant,
who was virtuous
and got up early,
my husband felt nothing for me.
He told his mother and father,
"I am leaving.
I can't live in the same house
with Isadasi."

Isadasi tried to live up to the ideal, acting towards her husband as a mother, a servant, and a slave. But despite her best effort, her marriage was neither successful nor happy. Her example, seen in the light of the various statements of the ideal, does provide us with a fairly clear picture of the wife's position. The ideal is called *patibbata* and is defined by Dhammapala as simply: "A woman who is entirely devoted to her husband and shows this behavior in her life."[5] Rather than being unique to Buddhism, this ideal is actually synonymous with the age-old Brahmanic ideal of *pativrata*, which is exemplified by women in classical Sanskrit literature, such as Sita, Radha, Savitri, Sati, and others.

Because the Buddhist cultural ideal of the wife does not diverge from the Brahmanic one, and because the Brahmanic ideal is the earlier of the two, ancient Brahmanic culture seems to be a good place to look for the source of the Buddhist ideal. In the earliest period of Aryan presence in India, a woman's status was comparatively high and she could fulfill her role by getting married and bearing sons. Indeed, in the Vedic age, the consummation of human life was not possible without marriage and family. The wife was known as *sahadharmini*, which meant that she was one with her husband. It was believed that the creator, Brahma, had divided his body into two parts, male and female, and thus a man and a woman could become perfect again only through marriage. As long as a man was without a wife or a woman without a husband, each was incomplete. Further, both husband and wife were necessary for the correct performance of religious rituals. Therefore, not only did the married woman take an active part in religious life; she was considered the source of *dharma* (law), *artha* (prosperity), and *kama* (love). She was her husband's best friend.

The relatively high standing of the married woman may have been possible because the Vedic-Aryans were a new people in a new land. A certain mutual reliance was necessary between men and women in order to survive. But as the Aryan race became established as the dominant people on the Indian subcontinent, the status of the wife declined.

Intermarriage between the Aryans and the indigenous races may have been a factor. Regardless of what caste an Aryan woman had belonged to, as Aryan men took non-Aryan, i.e. *sudra*, women as wives and lovers, the position of all women declined. All women came to be understood as belonging to the *sudra*, the lowest caste.

By the Buddhist period, the Brahmanic wife had neither the status and freedom she once had, nor was she yet weighed down by the oppressions of child-marriage, *purdah* (seclusion of women), and *sati* (widow-burning). Nonetheless, the groundwork for this later subjugation was being laid, and the ascendency of the renunciant ideal was partially to blame. Before considering the effect of renunciation on Buddhist marriages, however, a further comparison of Brahmanic and Buddhist marriages during the sixth century B.C.E. is in order.

A good source for information on Brahmanic marriages are the *Grihya Sutras*. Written in the sixth century B.C.E. , they are contemporary with the Pali Buddhist literature, and thus offer an excellent point of comparison. The *Grihya Sutras* identify eight forms of marriage.[6] The first four are "honorable"; the second four are "dishonorable." First is *brahma*, the most common form of Brahmanic marriage, in which the daughter is given to the bridegroom by the father. The bride is accompanied by a dowry. In the second form of marriage (*daiva*), the daughter is given to a brahman priest. The third form (*prajapatya*) is identical to the first, with the exception that a guardian, rather than the girl's father, arranges and gives the bride away. The forth form (*arsha*) is a mild form of bride purchase, in which the bride's father receives a pair of cattle in exchange for his daughter.

Of the dishonorable marriages, the first was love-marriage (*gandharva*). It was disapproved of because parents believed that young people did not have the discretion to make such important decisions. The next form of dishonorable marriage (*asura*) was bride-purchase. Often this form of marriage was a case of an older man acquiring a young, desirable wife. The seventh form of marriage (*paishacha*) was by drugging and/or rape of a woman. The last form of marriage (*rakshasa*), a form which, for the *kshattriya*, the warrior caste, could be a point of honor, was marriage by capture.

Just as in the Sanskrit literature, the *brahma* is the most common form of marriage among the women of the *Therigatha*. In this chapter, the marriage between Bhadda Kapilani and Kassapa is such an example; so is Isadasi's. In these marriages, equality of wealth is an important factor. However, we also find examples, in this and in earlier chapters, of marriages between spouses of differing wealth—the poverty-stricken Kisagotami is married to the son of a rich merchant; Bhadda Kundalakesa is allowed by her father to marry a thief.

The Pali literature classifies types of wives, rather than types of marriage. Though the subject under classification in the *Griyha Sutras* and the *Vinaya* differ somewhat, there is overlap, and each list serves to fill out the picture of the other. The lists in the Pali literature range from seven to ten types of wives, the most comprehensive of which, from the Patimokkha Laws of the *Vinaya*,[7] delineates all ten as follows:

> 1) *dhanakkita*—a woman bought with money for the purpose of sexual pleasure. She sells herself in order to obtain money.

> 2) *chandavasini*—a woman kept for passion. She stays with her husband of her own free will because she is one who lives for love.

> 3) *bhogavasini*—a woman who enjoys being a common housewife and who gets money in return.

> 4) *patavasini*—a woman who lives as a wife because she gains clothing. Such a woman has usually been poverty-stricken.

5) *odapattakini*—a woman who provides water. This type of wife is also in love and stays of her own free will.

6) *obhatacumbata*—a woman who formerly carried burdens, such as bundles of sticks, on her head. Such a wife is called "one who has taken off the pad" (*cumbataka*).

7) *dasi*—a slave woman who is taken by her master as his wife.

8) *kammakari*—a servant woman who is taken by her master as a wife.

9) *dhajahata*—a woman "brought by flag." Her husband, a warrior, has obtained her by force and made her his wife.

10) *muhuttiya*—a temporary wife, a wife for the moment.

The classification of marriages in the *Griyha Sutras* emphasizes honor and dishonor, right and wrong. What's right seems to be that which is done by the arrangement or with the authority of brahman men. The Vinaya list, however, gives a somewhat clearer picture of the woman herself, albeit of a wife who is often at the mercy of her husband's wealth, authority, or sexuality. On the basis of this picture, while it could hardly be said that the woman was "liberated" under Buddhism, at least her choices were no longer limited to her ability to produce sons, as they came to be under Brahmanism and later under Hinduism.

Whereas under Brahmanism the husband had rights and the woman had duties, a greater degree of mutuality was evident under Buddhism. Occasionally, the Buddha addressed teachings specifically to both husbands and wives, underlining the importance of mutual aid and respect. A husband should treat a wife in five ways—with respect, courtesy, faithfulness, by handing over household authority to her, and by providing her with adornments. In turn, a wife should perform her duties, be hospitable to kin, be faithful, watch over the goods he brings, and do her work with skill and industry.

In contrast to brides under Brahmanism, Buddhist women had greater scope in selecting their own partners. Love marriages were not frowned on and *svayambara* marriages, those in which the woman chose her husband from among a number of suitors, some-times occurred.

Monogamy was the marital ideal for followers of Brahmanism and Buddhism alike, but it was not always the practice. The Brahmanic attitude towards polygamy did not diverge from the Buddhist one. Polygamy was regarded with some complacence as the customary right of kings and other powerful men. The criterion for its accep-tance was whether or not a man could afford to keep more than one wife, that is, it was judged on practical rather than moral grounds. One justification for taking a second wife was the infertility of the first. Here the Brahmanic belief in the necessity of sons, a belief re-tained by many Buddhists, resurfaced. According to the Laws of Manu, a barren woman could be superseded in the eighth year, she whose children all die in the tenth year, and she who only bears daughters in the eleventh.[8] A wife's disobedience was another justi-fiable cause for a man's taking a second wife.

Whatever the reasons, in a polygamous marriage, the chief wife lived in the same house as her husband and was responsible for the management of her husband's affairs. Lesser wives and concubines lived in separate houses. The harem, discussed in the first chapter, consisted of the group of wives, lovers, female servants and slaves as-sociated with a particular man.

While for a man, the situation of having more than one wife might be a source both of satisfaction and status, for a woman it was usually a loathsome fate. As Kisagotami tells us, "to live with co-wives is suffering."[9] Thus, the condition earnestly desired by all wives was to "dwell at home without a rival."[10] And while some women gave consent to a second marriage, even these women usu-ally became jealous of their competition. So unhappy was the life of a co-wife that King Brahmadatta refused to give his daughter to a certain prince on the grounds that a woman's worst misery was to live among co-wives.[11]

Instances of polyandry—women having more than one hus-band—despite the exception of Drampadi in the Mahabharata, are rarely found in either the classical Sanskrit or Pali literature. Like-wise, the practice of a married woman committing adultery is almost unheard of, as a woman's chastity was strictly upheld. Among the Licchavis, a powerful tribe frequently visited by the Buddha, the punishment for a woman who broke her marriage vow was so severe that her husband could take her life with impunity. Examples of adulterous women, such as those in the *Jatakas*, seem to be the misogynist projections of celibate monks, rather than a source for information with a basis in fact.

Separation and divorce were generally forbidden under Brahmanism. The agreement to terminate one's marriage was permitted by the Buddhists, though the occurrence was rare. Buddhist widows could remarry the brother of a dead husband, as could wives whose husbands had left home to become renunciants. Neither of these circumstances of remarriage was allowed under Brahmanism. While *sati*, widow-burning, did not become commonplace until centuries after the Buddha's lifetime, the life of the Brahmanic widow was still severely restricted. And, while it was considered a disgrace for a woman to remain single according to Brahmanic values, this did not pertain to a Buddhist woman. She could be single and remain in her parents' home.

That the Buddha taught faithfulness and respect between spouses, and in addition, allowed women to remain single or divorce, is to his credit. Still, renunciation, not earthly or sacramental marriage, was the highest Buddhist aspiration. The renunciant ideal created its own set of problems, not only by breaking up a number of marriages, but by indirectly contributing to a virulent misogyny that was to take root in India in the centuries after the Buddha's death. The Buddha's own life story implicitly contradicts the Brahmanic valuation of marriage and having many sons as the *sine qua non* of the good life, and puts forth instead a new idea—the man who leaves wife and child to search for understanding. Such a man is "the conqueror," "the hero," "the sage." But why should this new idea, an ideal which women too could realize, lead to the increasing mistreatment of women? Examining this question, Nancy Falk speculates,

> Denigrating literature was produced by Buddhist monks. Such monks were expected to practice strict celibacy. Yet many were former householders who had known the pleasures of sexual intimacy. Some found its loss harder to bear than expected....Many of the most lurid portrayals of feminine wickedness were presented as a corrective to such immediate and practical situations [as a monk's desire to backslide].

Monks were expected not only to control their actions but also to weed out the very thought of wrong-doing. Freud has taught us much about the relationship between such radically repressed thoughts and excessive anxiety about their objects.[12]

The mistreatment of women was, unfortunately, not limited to denigrating literature produced by unenlightened monks. The threat posed by a husband's renunciation had a more immediate impact. More serious than the threat to a woman's self-esteem was the possibility that she might be abandoned. When a husband renounced the world, his wife had one of two courses to follow. She could either stay in the house or follow in the footsteps of her husband. In the *Mahavagga* we come across people saying, "Why has Gautama come here? To take away our sons and make our daughters widows!"[13]As one Indian woman scholar, Meena Talim, comments:

> From this we can presume that such women were considered widows and spent the rest of their life in exclusion. In a way their position was better than a widow. Such a woman could move in the house with the same dignity and authority even in the absence of her husband; but at the same time her lot was almost tragic, as she must have been constantly tortured by the thought that her husband, though living, heard not the promptings of her heart but ran off after spiritual elevation. Her self-respect must have been, on and off, wounded with re-membrance. Besides being thus emotionally wrecked, many women had to undergo economic crises.[14]

While a wife's consent was a prerequisite to a husband's renunciation, this did not seem to be an absolute rule. In the *Udana* we come across the pathetic story of the wife of Sangamaji. Sangamaji, having renounced the world to become a Buddhist monk, is depicted seated under a tree, strenuously seeking to gain enlightenment. Having brought her young child along and sought her husband out, the wife begs her former husband, "Oh mendicant, this is a small child. Nourish him." But the monk took no notice either of her or her heart-rending lamentations. So she set the child down in front of him, withdrew some distance and again pleaded, "Oh mendicant, this is your child. Nourish him." But again the monk paid no attention to her and out of motherly instinct, she picked up the child and, weeping over her helpless condition, returned home.

Meena Talim again comments in her own passionate English:

> One is shocked to see the Buddha, the Compassionate, praising the monk Sangamaji saying, "He is a real Brahmin, who feels no pleasure when she comes and no sorrow when she goes." Here the woman, at great cost putting aside her self-respect, asked a favor of her husband for mere maintenance. She went to take refuge in him, not as a husband but as a mere guardian and master of the house. Therefore one cannot resist pondering—was Buddha justified in praising such a monk and were such men justified in embracing recluse life shirking family responsibilities?[15]

The stories and poems of the nuns who had formerly been wives leave the reader with the impression that their marriages were a struggle. The nuns had been unhappy wives, and their poems are the female equivalent of the much more extensive literature by monks, expressing discontent with both their spouses and their lives as householders.

The story of Bhadda Kapilani in this chapter is an exception. It comes closest to the Buddhist ideal, not of marriage, but of renunciation. Brought together by the arrangement of their parents, Bhadda Kapilani and Kassapa decide on their wedding night not to consummate their marriage but to renounce the world together. The last poem in this chapter is a rare example of the conflict which broke up a marriage and a husband's decision to renounce the world. While the intimate scene is one of pain, there is a quality of tenderness in the resolution—the husband agreeing to carry his wife's offering to the Buddha. These and the other stories and poems in this chapter give us a living picture of the role of the wife and the condition of married life in ancient Buddhist India.

BHADDA KAPILANI

Bhadda Kapilani, the legend goes, had many lives and knew them all. And many of those lives were intertwined with a certain man. His name was Kassapa and he was famous as one of the greatest disciples of the Buddha. Bhadda is less well known; this is her story.

Incalculable eons ago, in the time of Padumattara Buddha, Bhadda heard of a female renunciant who could recall her former lives. She resolved to acquire that same power and Kassapa, her husband, resolved to live a life of austerity. Later, in the time of Vipassi Buddha, these two were again married and belonged to the brahman caste. In a later lifetime still, the same two were tribespeople. In that life, after a quarrel with her sister-in-law, Bhadda offered a bowl of food to a *pacceka buddha* (one who, though enlightened, refrained from teaching others) and prayed, "May I have a shining body like this offering."

In her life contemporary with that of Siddhartha Gautama, Bhadda Kapilani was born into a wealthy family of the Kosiya clan. She grew up in Sagala, the capital of the kingdom of Madda. One day as a child, she saw crows eating some insects that were wriggling among drying sesame seeds. The sight distressed the sensitive child, but even more distressing was when some adults told her that the insects' death was due to her own sin. This seemingly trivial but significant incident shaped her later decision to renounce the world.

A similar incident influenced the boy who was one day to become her husband. When Kassapa, standing in a freshly plowed field, saw worms being eaten by some birds, he too was led to believe that he was to blame for that suffering. Like Bhadda, he resolved to become a renunciant when he grew up.

As their independently-arrived-at decision to renounce the world naturally precluded sexuality, marriage, and children, both Bhadda and Kassapa assumed they would never marry. But this choice upset Kassapa's parents so much that he eventually agreed to marry on the condition that the woman his parents chose resemble a statue he would make. The statue was made and messengers were sent throughout the land to search for the living match. Amazingly, Bhadda was found. Then the two sets of parents began secretly to arrange the marriage. When the young bridal pair found out about the arrangements, they tried to sabotage them, writing each other letters about what terrible spouses they would be. But the letters were intercepted and the marriage took place anyway.

Privately, Bhadda and Kassapa agreed not to consummate the marriage, but instead to renounce the world together. They cut off each other's hair, donned saffron-colored clothes from their vast wardrobes, granted freedom to their slaves, and set off into home-lessness. Kassapa walked in front, Bhadda behind, but they quickly realized this was not appropriate. Reading this story today with our own cultural biases, we might suppose that they were operating un-der democratic assumptions expressed in Buddhist terms—everyone is equal before the Dharma. But in fact, the man walking in front, the woman behind signified marriage. There was the contradiction. Were they married or renunciant? Thus, when they came to a cross-roads, they resolved the matter by parting, he taking the right fork, she the left.

Within a brief time, Kassapa encountered the Buddha and was given ordination. But Bhadda's course was more difficult. At least five years would pass before the early Buddhist sect summoned the revolutionary spirit the Jains had already displayed and permitted the formation of an order of nuns. Meanwhile, Bhadda lived near the Jeta Grove at Savatthi waiting, and when Pajapati established the first community of nuns, Bhadda joined her, received full ordination, and attained the great peace she sought.

> Kassapa, the Buddha's son and heir,
> deep meditator,
> knows that he has lived before,
> sees heaven and hell
> and won't be born again.
> He is a sage who has attained the highest
> knowledge.
>
> In just this same way
> Bhadda Kapilani
> with the same three knowledges
> has left death behind
> and bears her last body.
>
> We saw the misery in the world,
> the two of us,
> and turned away from home.
> Now we have finished

with mind's obsessions
and are both grown gentle,
quenched and cool.

MUTTA

Mutta was the daughter of a poor brahman family. Confined by her family's poverty and by the custom of marrying within one's caste, she was married to a hunch-backed brahman through the arrangements of her parents. The detail of his crooked back was less significant than the unhappiness of the marriage itself. When this unhappiness became apparent to all, Mutta convinced her husband, whose permission was necessary, that she be allowed to ordain as a Buddhist nun. This accomplished, she took up her new life with great sincerity and eventually became an *arahant*.

An interesting term in Mutta's poem is the word "*muttiya*." Though this has previously been translated into English as "freedom from," it more accurately means "free by the means of." By this rendering, a more subtle point than mere complaint is expressed. The things that formerly oppressed Mutta are not merely what she has happily renounced. Instead, the aspects of her former "oppression" are in fact the means of her release.[16]

> Free, I am free.
> I am free
> by means of the three
> crooked things,
> mortar, pestle, and
> my crooked husband.
>
> I am free
> from birth and death
> and all that dragged me back.

AN ANONYMOUS WIFE

This woman was born and married within the brahman caste. When Gautama came to her town, Vesali, she was impressed by his teaching and became a lay disciple. Later, she heard Pajapati preach and wanted to join her community. But her husband withheld his consent, and so she continued to live out her obligations as a brahman wife and, as best as she could, to devote herself to a lay discipleship.

One day, as she was in the kitchen cooking curry, the meal caught fire, and with a great crackling, was consumed by flames. In that moment, she had a deep insight into the Buddhist teaching of impermanence. This established her on the third stage of the path.[17] From then on she decided to wear no more jewels or ornaments, observing a precept applicable to one who has already received ordination. When her husband asked about this, she told him she was incapable of living a domestic life. So together husband and wife went to Pajapati and the wife became a nun.

Although the *Therigatha* Commentary speaks of this anonymous nun as a devoted wife, the story gives another impression—of a woman who preferred the life of renunciation to that of marriage. Nonetheless, her experience of insight occurs in the context of her domestic life. This parallels Mutta's experience, whom we have seen is freed by the means of mortar, pestle, and husband.

The Buddha used this wife's experience as the basis for the theme in the following brief poem. When the anonymous wife had attained complete enlightenment, the poem is said to have become her own.

> Sleep sweetly, dear sister
> in the robe you made.
> Your desire is still,
> like dried up vegetables
> in a pot.

SUMANGALA'S MOTHER

Here is another anonymous wife, known to us only as a woman of a poor family of Savatthi, the wife of a basket maker, and the mother of Sumangala, a Buddhist monk.

Of all the wives' poems, hers expresses the strongest loathing of domesticity. Sumangala's mother is so vehemently opposed to her domestic life that she engenders in the reader an opposite emotion, humor. Her disgust is so complete that her situation seems to us rather comical.

Free, I am free!
How glad I am to be free
from my pestle.
My cooking pot seems
worthless to me.
And I can't even bear
to look at his sun-umbrella—
my husband disgusts me!

So I destroy greed and hate
with a sizzle.
And I am the same woman
who goes to the foot of a tree
and says to herself,
"Ah, happiness,"
and meditates with happiness.

CAPA

With marital strife so common in our own era, it is fascinating to uncover a poem 2,500 years old dealing with the same theme. Capa's story is in fact the story of her marriage to and separation from Kala.

Kala had been an ascetic of the Ajivaka school prior to meeting Capa. The Ajivaka's revered leader and guiding light was a man named Makkhali Gosala, a contemporary of Siddhartha Gautama. Makkhali Gosala and Gautama were two among numerous religious teachers in the Ganges region during that era. Kala's connection to Siddhartha Gautama was that he was the first person whom the Buddha encountered after his enlightenment. Meeting this fellow-traveler on the road to Kasi, Kala questioned the Buddha about his insight, asking if he were an *anantajina*, the Ajivaka term for a buddha.

"Yes I am," Siddhartha Gautama replied, and went on to say:

All conquering, all knowing am I.
In all dharmas untainted.
Giving up all,
free from wanting,

having become enlightened by myself,
who may I point out?

I have no teacher;
there is no one like me.
I have no peer in the world
or among the gods.

I am an *arahant* in the world.
I am the unsurpassed teacher.
I alone am the fully enlightened one.
I have become cool, quenched.[18]

Noncommittal, Kala replied, "It may be so, friend," and went along another road.

Shortly thereafter, Kala came to the country of Vankahara, in the district of Nala, where Capa lived. She was the daughter of a trapper. Capa's father, kindly disposed towards this wandering ascetic, began to regularly provide Kala with almsfood. One day, when Capa's father and other trappers were heading off on a long hunt, he told Capa to look after the ascetic. When Kala made his almsround that day, he saw Capa and immediately fell in love with her, privately vowing that he would fast until death if he could not have her as his wife.

When Capa's father returned six days later and inquired after the ascetic, he learned that Kala had come for almsfood the first day, but had not returned. Concerned, the trapper went out in search of him. When he found the gaunt ascetic and heard of Kala's vow, the trapper consented to the marriage of the ascetic and his daughter on the condition that the ascetic learn to hunt.

Capa and Kala lived together happily for a time, and during that period, they had a child. But later their relationship became strained; she would provoke him and he would threaten to leave, always holding on to the memory of the person he met on the road to Kasi who said he was an *anantajina*. Eventually, the couple's fighting came to a head. The poem that follows records their intimate crisis and separation.

Capa is clearly threatened by the thought that she and her child might be abandoned. In her vulnerability, she falls back on her power as a woman, first trying the tact of submissiveness. She says, "I'll be your slave."[19] Failing there, she tries to win Kala over by seduction, but this approach is lost on the aspiring ascetic. As a last resort, Capa tries to appeal to him through their son. But this too is unsuccessful, and next we see a remarkable and sudden shift, as though having tried absolutely everything, Capa must and does let go. ("Then good-bye Kala. Where will you go?") Suddenly there is a surprising tenderness to her words. And while, in the course of the mounting battle, the reader may feel increasingly angry at Kala's insensitivity, by the end of the poem, the reader senses the poignancy in Kala's act of carrying Capa's offering to the Buddha. It is as though by this act he communicates both his love for Capa and his need for independence, qualities he could not express in the marriage. With this, our possible anger at Kala turns to an acknowledgment of things as they are, of people as they are.

Broken-hearted after his departure, Capa leaves the child with her father and follows after Kala, not to get him back, but to meet the Buddha herself. This she does at Savatthi. There she receives ordination, and later she becomes an *arahant*.

[Kala:]

Once I was an ascetic with a stick in hand.
Now I am a deer hunter.
It's because of my own lust
that I'm in this swamp
and can't see my way clear
to the other shore.
Capa thinks I love her;
she has kept our son happy.
But I want to cut my ties with her
and renounce the world again.

[Capa:]

Great man, don't be angry with me!
Wise man, don't be angry with me!

How can you be pure or austere
when you are controlled by your anger?

[Kala:]

I'm really going to leave!
Who'd want to live in Nala?
Here women use their bodies to trap ascetics
who only want to live the Dharma.

[Capa:]

Kala, come back!
Enjoy my love.
I'll be your slave
and all my relatives too.

[Kala:]

If even a part of what you say were true,
Capa,
that would be terrific for
someone who was turned on by you.

[Capa:]

Oh Kala,
I am like a Takkara tree
blossoming on a mountain top,
like a bitter-apple vine in flower,
like a trumpet flower in the interior of an island.
My body has been rubbed
with golden sandalwood paste.[20]
I have put on muslin from Varanasi.
I am beautiful.
Why do you leave me?

[Kala:]

You are like a bird-hunter
with that lovely body of yours,
but you won't snare me.

[Capa:]

But Kala,
this child-fruit of mine is yours.
How can you leave me when I have your child?

[Kala:]

The wise leave their sons,
their relatives, and their wealth.
The great set out
like an elephant that has broken its tether.

[Capa:]

Then I'll knock him into the dirt —
right here!
this son of yours,
with a stick! with a knife!
And out of grief you won't go.

[Kala:]

Even if you give our son to the jackals and dogs
I won't turn back, poor woman.

[Capa:]

Then good-bye, Kala.
Where will you go?
To a village, a town, a city, a capital?

[Kala:]

Once we had followers.
We wandered from village to village,
to cities and capitals.
We thought we were ascetics,
but we weren't.
But now by the Neranjara River
the Buddha teaches the Dharma to the living.
I'll go to him;
he'll be my teacher.

[Capa:]

> Then give him my greetings,
> the guide of the world,
> and make an offering for me.

[Kala:]

> It's right, what you say Capa.
> I'll give him your greeting,
> the guide of the world,
> and make an offering for you.

> * * *

> Then Kala went to the Neranjara River
> and saw the Enlightened One
> teaching "no death"[21]—

> pain,
> the cause of pain,
> the end of pain,
> and the great eightfold way[22]
> that stills all pain.

> Kala bowed to his feet,
> walked past him on the right,
> made the offering for Capa,
> then set out into homelessness.

> The three knowledges have been realized.[23]
> The Buddha's teaching has been done.

---

[1] I.B. Horner, tr. *The Book of Discipline*. Vol. I. (London: Oxford University Press Warehouse, 1938), p. 140.

[2] Richard Morris, ed. *The Book of Gradual Sayings*. (*Anguttara Nikaya*.) Vol. IV. (London: Pali Text Society), pp. 265-266.

[3] Meena Talim. *Women in Early Buddhist Literature*. (Bombay: University of Bombay Press, 1972), p. 136.

[4] Original poem from Richard Pischel. *The Therigatha*. (London: Pali Text Society, 1966), p. 163. Because this is a late poem and because I have limited the poems in the chapters proper to women who were probable contemporaries of the Buddha, this excerpt from Isadasi's long poem has been woven into the chapter introduction in order that readers might enjoy it as well.

[5] Meena Talim. *Op. Cit.*, p. 133.

[6] Shakuntala Rao Shastri. *Women in the Vedic Age*. (Calcutta: Bharatiya Vidya Bhavan, 1969), p. 129-130.

[7] F.L. Woodward, tr. *The Book of Gradual Sayings*. (Anguttata Nikaya) Vol. I-V (London: Pub. for the Pali Text Society by Oxford University Press, 1932-1936), Vol. IV. p. 92.

[8] Prof. Indra. *Status of Women in Ancient India*. (Banaras: Motilal Banarasidass, 1955), p. 61.

[9] See Chapter Five, Kisagotami poem.

[10] I.B. Horner. *Women Under Primitive Buddhism*. (London: George Routledge and Sons, Ltd., 1930. Rep. by Asia Book Corporation, 1975), p. 37.

[11] Meena Talim. *Op. Cit.*, p. 133.

[12] Nancy Falk. "An Image of Women in Old Buddhist Literature" in *Women and Religion*. Judith Plaskow and Joan Arnold, ed. (Missoula, Montana: Scholars Press, 1974), p. 108.

[13] Meena Talim. *Op. Cit.*, p. 130.

[14] *Ibid.*, p. 130.

[15] *Ibid.*, p. 128.

[16] In the collection of monks poems, the *Theragatha*, we find that a poem by Sumangala is almost identical to Mutta's, only his expression of loathing is for the sickle, plow, and spade; that is to say, for the back-breaking work of a peasant farmer.

[17] The third stage of the path is also called the stage of never-returning. For a full description of all four stages, see *marga* in the glossary.

[18] Roger Milliken, tr. Unpublished manuscript.

[19] The best wife resembles a mother, sister, friend, or slave, according to the *Anguttara* IV. 92. (F.L. Woodward, tr. *Op Cit*.)

[20] Sandalwood rubbed into wet paste was one of the many coolants and cleansers in great demand. It was a necessity rather than a luxury in a hot climate where soap had not yet been invented.

[21] *Amatam padam* is a synonym of *nirvana*. It is the state where there is no more birth or death. *Amata* literally means the drink of the gods, *padam* literally means the region or place of that drink.

[22] Four Noble Truths (*ariya-sacca*) and eightfold way (*ariya-atthangika-magga*) under *ariya-sacca*. See glossary.

[23] *Tevijja*—three knowledges. See glossary.

CHAPTER SEVEN

Old Women

The women of this chapter share the characteristic of being old. Age in itself doesn't make them *theris*. *Theri* can mean old woman, but in the title of the *Therigatha* it means a woman having seniority in the Buddhist order of nuns, having spent twelve years in the sangha, and/or a nun distinguished for her character and wisdom.

While the Buddha taught respect for the elders of the order, both male and female, old age itself was not necessarily revered in sixth century B.C.E. Indian culture. In his first sermon delivered at the Deer Park, Gautama spoke of old age as one of the aspects of suffering, along with birth, sickness, and death. Not only was old age an aspect of suffering; being an old woman could be a particular burden. Physically a woman was no longer beautiful. We find the image of an old woman frequently used as a symbol of impermanence and decay. A story from the *Dhammapada* Commentary is a rather cruel example:

> The story goes that this nun continued her alms-pilgrimages until she was a hundred and twenty years old. One day as she was returning from her alms-pilgrimage with food in her bowl, she met a certain monk in the street. She asked permission of him to give him the food in her bowl, and he consented to accept it. So she gave him all she had, and then she had none. On the second day and again on the third day she met the same monk in the same place, gave him all the food she had, and then had none left for herself.
>
> Now on the fourth day, as she was going on her round, she met the Teacher in a certain place which was much more crowded. She stepped back, and as she did so, the skirt of her robe slipped down and she trod on it. Unable to keep her feet, she tumbled and fell down. The Teacher came up to her and said, "Sister, your body is worn out with old age; at a time not far distant it will suffer dissolution." So saying, he pronounced the following stanza,
>
> "This body is worn out, this nest of disease, this fragile body;
> This mass of corruption dissolves, for life ends in death."[1]

If, in fact, the Buddha did say this, one imagines that he said it in kindness and compassion, as a doctor can be kind when he truthfully tells a patient she will die. Though a wrenching story, it is presented as an example of how old age was viewed not as a noble, but as a wretched state.

In its early days, the order of nuns did not serve specifically as a refuge for old women and widows. Rather—and the range of ages of the women in the *Therigatha* supports this—women of all ages and walks of life entered the community. In the centuries to come, after the sangha of ordained nuns had practically died out, nuns were no longer given full ordination, and nunneries of some Southeast Asian countries were increasingly comprised of old women and widows. They shaved their heads, kept eight or ten precepts rather than the three hundred and eleven of the original nuns' sangha, and lived in special sections of the monasteries or in their own convents. In Burma, for example, the majority of nuns have been old women, typically widows. In Cambodia, widows would mourn their husbands as Buddhist nuns for three years following the husband's death.

Of the three women we meet in this chapter, only Dhamma is clearly identified as a widow. The marital status of Citta and Sumana is not mentioned, though they may have been widows, since single women were exceptional. The customs a widow was expected to observe were austere, though the Buddhist widows were somewhat better off than their Brahmanic counterparts.

For Brahmanic widows, their position in the Vedic period was better than in the sixth century B.C.E. *Sati*, a word descriptive of a chaste woman, was commonly used to refer to a woman who casts herself on her husband's funeral pyre (a practice not authorized in the Vedas). Widows could and did remarry. By the Buddhist period, Brahmanic widows had to practice austerities, eating frugally and fasting at specific times, shaving their heads like renunciants, not wearing bright clothing or jewels, and sleeping on mats on the floor. Remarriage was strictly forbidden to them, though this was not true for the widower. *Sati*, if it existed at all, was still very rare. It is in the Epic period (200 B.C.E.-200 C.E.) that we begin to find instances of a widow's self-immolation, and by the Smrti period (400-700 C.E.) *sati* was highly applauded and commonly practiced. It was by then considered the surest way of redeeming the widow's soul.

The Buddhist widow was much better off. She did not have to practice austerities. Also, remarriage was allowed, though we hear of almost no examples, which suggests that the Brahmanic custom probably held sway. Women did, however, have the right of inheritance. Yet despite the relatively greater liberties and rights allowed Buddhist widows compared to Brahmanic widows, their status was still not high. The adjective *anatha*, meaning "destitute" or "unprotected," is used to describe the widow's condition. It is also used to describe an unmarried woman, suggesting that the two groups shared a similar marginality within their society.

Another story from the *Dhammapada* Commentary is about a Buddhist widow, Bahuputtika, and it gives a picture of what such a woman's life could be like:

> In a certain household at Savatthi, we are told, were seven sons and seven daughters. All of them married as soon as they were old enough, and were happy, as was indeed their nature. After a time their father died. But the mother, the eminent lay disciple, even after the death of her husband, did not for some time relinquish control of his property. One day her sons said to her, "Mother, now that our father is dead, what is the use of your retaining his property? Can we not support you?" She listened to their words, but said nothing. After they had spoken to her several times about the matter, she thought to herself, "My sons will look after me; why need I keep the property separate for myself?" So she divided the estate into two parts and distributed them among her children.
>
> After a few days had passed, the wife of her oldest son said to her: "Apparently this is the only house our excellent mother visits; she acts as though she had given both parts of her estate to her oldest son." In like manner did the wives of her other sons address her. So likewise did her daughters address her whenever she entered their houses, from the oldest to the youngest. With such disrespect was she treated that finally she said to herself, "Why should I live with them any longer? I will enter the Order and live the life of a nun." So she went to the nuns' convent and asked to be admitted. They received her into the Order, and when she had made her full profession she went by the name of Bahuputtika the nun.
>
> "Since I have entered the Order in my old age," thought she, as she performed the major and minor duties assigned to

nuns, "it behooves me to be diligent; I will therefore spend the whole night in meditation." On the lower terrace, putting her hand on a pillar, she guided her steps and meditated. Even as she walked along, fearful that in the dark she might strike her head against a tree or against some other object, she put her hand on a tree and guided her steps. Resolved to observe only the Law taught by the Teacher, she considered the Law, pondered the Law and meditated.

The Teacher, seated in the Perfumed Chamber, sent forth a radiant image of himself, and sitting as if face to face with her, talked with her saying, "Bahuputtika, though one should live a hundred years, did she not behold the Law I have taught and meditate thereon, it were better that she live but a moment and behold the Law I have taught..." At the conclusion... Bahuputtika became an Arahant possessed of the Supernatural Powers.[2]

Just as it did for Bahuputtika, the order of nuns would have offered old women an opportunity to begin a new life. The three women we meet in this chapter show us different faces of old age. Dhamma comes to insight through seeing the misery of old age. Citta struggles against her age and is proud of her physical stamina and energy. And Sumana, having longed to be a nun over a period of years, shows a certain mellowness and ease in her old age.

DHAMMA

Dhamma was from a respectable family and married a respectable husband. When she heard the Buddha teach, she wanted to become a nun, but could not receive the necessary permission from her husband. In an act of devotion typical of and highly respected in an Indian wife, she did not disobey. Rather, she waited until her husband's death and then became ordained. Her realization experience happened one day when, returning to the hermitage after almsround, she lost her balance and fell.

> I wandered for alms.
> I leaned on a stick.
> My whole body was weak
> and trembled.

Suddenly I fell down
and could see clearly
the misery of this body.
My heart was freed.

CITTA

In Rajagaha, Citta was born into a well-to-do family. It was hearing
Gautama's teaching at the gate of Rajagaha that led her to seek ordination by Pajapati. Yet it was not until her old age that she gained
the insight she sought. This breakthrough occurred one day when
she had climbed Vulture Peak and done the usual exercises of a
recluse.

Though Vulture Peak was not a high mountain, it required some
stamina to ascend. It consisted mostly of rock, and was named for
the formation at the top which resembled a vulture's head. From the
top, Citta would have seen a beautiful, wide view of rolling, craggy
hills and a dense forest below.

Though I am thin, sick,
and lean on a stick,
I have climbed up Vulture Peak.

Robe thrown down,
bowl turned over,
leaned on a rock,
then great darkness opened.

SUMANA

Sumana was considered by the Buddha to be among the eminent lay
disciples. Although she wanted to become a nun, she had to postpone her wish in order to care for her aging grandmother, who had
been like a mother to her and her brother, Pasenadi, king of Kosala.
Despite her responsibilities, she would be present whenever
Gautama came to teach in her brother's court. Later, after her grandmother passed away, Sumana and her brother went together to
Pajapati's community to request Sumana's ordination. By this time,
Sumana was an old woman. Yet, so ripe was she after years of

a devoted lay discipleship, that on that very day, simply hearing the Buddha's sermon, she experienced immediate and complete realization.

This is the poem that brought her to that realization. Though spoken initially by the Buddha, the poem was said to have become her own after she attained *nirvana*.

> Lie down, old woman
> in the robe you made.
> Your desire is still.
> You are quenched and cool.

---

[1] E.W. Burlingame. *Buddhaghosa's "Dhammapada" Commentary (Dhammapadatthakatha)*. 3 Vols. Harvard Oriental Series, Vol. 28. (Cambridge: Harvard University Press, 1921), p. 334.

[2] *Ibid.*, pp. 260-261.

CHAPTER EIGHT

Prostitutes, Courtesans, & Beautiful Women

In India, since time immemorial, the prostitute, courtesan, or beautiful woman has been opposed to the male renunciant. From a Western psychological point of view, this pair would be seen as only superficially in opposition. Each is the shadow of the other; each requires the other. But a renunciant tradition like Buddhism has a different perspective on sensuality and celibacy. From a Buddhist point of view, the tension between the renunciant monk and the sensuous woman is transcended by the negation of the feminine aspect. We see this played out in Buddhist art and legend.

In early Buddhist art, women are invariably depicted sensuously. They are large-breasted and wide-hipped; their stance and gestures are inviting. The prototype are the *asparas*, "heavenly beings" belonging to a pantheon of folk deities. These temptresses are carved on the gates at Bharut and Sanchi (second—first century B.C.E.), famous sites of early Buddhist art. It is through these gates that the devotee must pass in order to enter the Buddhist temple compound. The metaphor is explicit—one must pass through the world of *samsara*, of birth and rebirth, of seduction by women, in order to reach the holy place where desire and temptation no longer exist.

While this imagery may or may not be central to a man's psychological or religious journey to wholeness, it does not have this role in a woman's journey, nor does it acknowledge particular women who might be victimized by this mythology. This chapter seeks to go beneath the imagery projected onto beautiful or sensuous women, by letting the women themselves express their sexuality and religion, through their own stories and poems .

The title of this chapter is meant to show something of the range into which this group of women can be divided. Prostitutes comprise the first subgroup. Then as now, prostitutes were women who earned their livelihood by offering their bodies for indiscriminate sexual intercourse. The word for prostitute in Pali is *vesi* or *vesiya*. It literally means "a woman of low caste, a prostitute, a harlot." Her present day equivalent is the hooker or streetwalker. Such women probably did not amass great fortunes, nor were they the favored lovers of rich and powerful men. Vimala, whose story and poem are the first in this chapter, was such a woman, her mother having been a prostitute before her.

A description of a brothel from the *Dhammapada* Commentary gives us a glimpse into the prostitute's world:

> Out of every thousand pieces of money they received, five hundred were for the women, five hundred were the price of clothes, perfumes and garlands; the men who visited that house received garments to clothe themselves in, and stayed the night there; then on the next day they put off the garments they had received, and put on those they had brought and went their ways.[1]

A second subgroup consists of courtesans. Courtesans were a special class of prostitutes whose clientele was drawn from the court or wealthy class. Their present-day equivalent is the call girl. Ambapali and Addhakasi from this chapter are examples of such women. The fortunes they amassed could be fabulous, as great as the daily revenue of an entire city. Famous capitals like Vesali and Rajagaha had state-installed courtesans. Ambapali, for example, was the chief courtesan of Vesali. Such a woman would not only manage great sums of money, but a number of women as well.

Beautiful women are the third subgroup in this chapter. Though there are women renowned for their beauty throughout this book, a number of beautiful women are grouped together in this chapter because they share with prostitutes and courtesans the trait of physical attractiveness. Due to their beauty, rather than any self-chosen orientation, such women often became associated with seductive women. They were made into sex objects because of their beauty.

The beautiful woman of early Buddhist culture is not the equivalent to the fair damsel of medieval legend or to the goddess of Love, Aphrodite, of Greek mythology. She is closer to a type represented by Circe in the *Odyssey*, seductive and forbidding. While beauty was generally held in esteem in ancient India, and while one of the traditional blessings in Buddhist scripture was for beauty, there was also a dark and negative quality about a woman's beauty.

A beautiful woman was seen as dangerous: dangerous to herself, dangerous to a man, and certainly dangerous to a monk. She was a

danger to herself because she could become attached to her loveliness. Thus, under Buddhism the woman was instructed to observe
the rotting and decay of her body, or to meditate on corpses. We find
examples of this practice in the chapter ahead.

A beautiful woman was dangerous to men for the obvious reason
that a man would desire her. As cutting out the root of desire was
the aspiration of all Buddhists, such a woman might pose an insurmountable temptation. Furthermore, women were believed to have
an insatiable sexual drive. The scriptures speak of four things that
are insatiable: the ocean, kings, brahmans, and a woman's lust. A
Dhammapada story describes the numerous ways in which a woman
accosts a man due to her insatiable sexual energy:

> She yawns, she bows down, she makes amorous gestures, she
> pretends to be abashed, she rubs the nails of one hand or foot
> with the nails of the other hand or foot, she places one foot
> on the other foot, she scratches on the ground with a stick.
> She causes her man to leap up, she causes her man to leap
> down, she dallies with her man, and makes him dally with her,
> she kisses him and makes him kiss her, she eats food and makes
> him eat food, she gives and begs for gifts, she imitates what-
> ever he does. She talks in a loud tone, she talks in a low tone;
> she talks as in public, she talks as in private. While dancing,
> singing, playing musical instruments, weeping, making amo-
> rous gestures, adorning herself, she laughs and looks. She
> sways her hips, she jiggles her waist-gear, she uncovers her
> thigh, covers her thigh, displays her breast, displays her arm-
> pit, and displays her navel. She buries the pupils of her eyes,
> lifts her eyebrows, scratches her lips and dangles her tongue.
> She takes off her loin-cloth, puts on her loin-cloth, takes off
> her turban, and puts on her turban.[2]

If we examine the words women use to describe themselves, they
don't indicate an obsession with sexual desire. The women of this
chapter, presumably the ones with the most insatiable drives, refer
to their desire no more frequently than other women in the
Therigatha, nor more often than monks in the *Theragatha*. When we
try to pinpoint the source for this assumption of women's insatiable
sexual desire, we find it, in fact, to be the obsession of men, particularly of male renunciants. Kala, Capa's former husband, shows this

bias in a poem from Chapter Six. "I'm really going to leave! / Who'd want to live in Nala? / Here women use their bodies to trap ascetics / who only want to live by the Dharma."

Whereas Buddhist monks are frequently haunted by images of women, or shaken in their resolve by thoughts of wives or lovers, the nuns do not speak of a comparable temptation by former husbands or lovers. The impression is that, when these women had strong sexual feelings, they didn't project them outwards or blame men for them. Equally striking, the prostitutes', courtesans', and beautiful women's self-images do not seem to be based on extremes of fascination and loathing. When these women speak of their former profession or of their beauty, they do so straightforwardly. They seem comparatively at ease with themselves and with their sexuality. Consequently, they appear to be at ease with their decision to become renunciants, without needing to express derision of the opposite sex like some of the most esteemed Buddhist monks, including the Buddha himself on occasion.

The quintessential example of women's seduction is from the Buddha legend. When the Buddha resolves to sit under the Bodhi tree and remain there until he has attained the supreme wisdom, Mara, the Lord of Death and Desire, tries to attack the Buddha with his demonic armies. When this fails, Mara brings out his ultimate weapon, his three daughters, appropriately named Craving, Discontent, and Lust, women of unutterable beauty and seductive powers. When the Buddha remains unmoved by them, his enlightenment becomes a certainty.

Now the dependency of the male renunciant on the prostitute, courtesan, or beautiful woman is more apparent. She is the necessary foil to his purity. In early Buddhism, a sharp line was drawn between two states of existence, *nirvana* ("extinction") and *samsara* ("becoming"), a perpetual wandering from rebirth to rebirth. *Samsara* was the enemy. It had to be overcome for the desired extinction to occur. "Woman" was the veritable image of the blind urge towards "becoming" that was tantamount to *samsara*. That a woman never tired of two things, intercourse and childbearing, was a reflection of her nature. Nancy Falk writes, "She was the enemy—not only on a personal level as an individual source of temptation, but on the cosmic level as representation and summation of the processes binding all men."[3]

Having considered the relationship between the sensuous woman and the male renunciant, we should also look at the relationship between the prostitute or courtesan and the nun. These two seemingly opposed groups shared certain common traits vis-à-vis their society at large. Prostitutes and nuns both possessed a degree of independence that was unimaginable for most women. Neither had active male guardians; both moved relatively freely in the public sphere. Even the legal codes of the period grouped prostitutes and courtesans with nuns. Crimes against such women were equivalent before the law and less severely punished than those against other women.[4]

Several stories from the *Vinaya* point out a tension between the sexually promiscuous women and the nuns. Following the rape of a nun when she was bathing alone, a rule was made that nuns could only bathe at public bathing places. At one such place some nuns had occasion to bathe with prostitutes. Normally all Indian women shaved off their pubic hair; the only ones who did not observe this custom were prostitutes and nuns. On one occasion, seeing the nuns bathing naked, the prostitutes taunted the nuns for being just like them.[5] On another occasion at a public bathing site, some prostitutes mocked the nuns by saying, "Why are you young women living the holy life? Why not enjoy pleasure now and renounce the world when you are old? Then you can experience both."[6]

These are some examples drawn from ancient Indian iconography and scripture that show the relationship of prostitutes, courtesans, and beautiful women to Buddhist monks or nuns. We turn now to the individual women of this chapter for whom both dimensions, the sexual and the ascetic, were integral to their lives and to their particular paths to self-knowledge.

VIMALA

Vimala was the daughter of a prostitute. When she grew up, she followed her mother's trade.

A story survives of her life as a young prostitute. One day in Vesali, Vimala encountered Moggallana. Whether she knew of his status as a leading monk under Gautama or not, it is said that she went to his dwelling place and tried to seduce him. Her attempt failed completely—Moggallana proved a model renunciant and spurned her in these words:

> You bag of dung, tied up with skin. You demoness with lumps on your breast. The nine streams in your body flow all the time, are vile smelling, and full of dung. A monk desiring purity avoids your body as one avoids dung.[7]

This is the language of a man whom, along with Sariputta, Gautama described in this way, "Outstanding they are among my disciples; exceptional they are among my disciples."[8] Although no record has been preserved of Vimala's response, we do know that this interaction marked a change in her life. She became a Buddhist lay disciple, then an ordained nun, and ultimately an arahant.

This might strike us as odd—why would Vimala become a Buddhist on the basis of such a crude put-down? This relates again to the interdependence of the renunciant and the prostitute, in Indian culture generally, and in the Theravadin Buddhist system specifically.

Theravadin Buddhism, with its goal of subduing sensual pleasure and its elevation of the status of the celibate monk or nun, inadvertently sets sexuality in opposition to religious accomplishment. Under such a system, a model renunciant who speaks and acts as Moggallana did to Vimala becomes the hero. Yet the hero needs an enemy. Each is incomplete without the other. How is Moggallana incomplete? Moggallana falls short in his cruel and self-protecting response to Vimala. His words reveal a person attached to his purity, one who has externalized all negativity.

A Zen koan takes up this same theme but with a different outcome:

> An old woman provided alms to a certain monk for twenty years. One day she sent her sixteen-year-old niece with the almsfood and instructions. The girl laid her head on the old monk's lap and said, "How is this?"
>
> The monk replied, "A withered tree is rooted in an ancient rock. It is without warmth, without life."

> When the girl returned, she told the old woman what had happened. "You hypocrite!" the old woman cried out, and she drove the monk away and burned down his hut.[9]

While we may question the use of the niece as bait to test the monk's realization, his response is recognized by the old woman as aloof and defensive. On the other hand, she was not looking for the monk to take the niece up on her invitation. For the old woman, an appropriate answer would acknowledge that sexuality exists, but would neither revile the girl nor make her into a sex object.

Unlike either Moggallana or the monk in the Zen koan, many monks speak of a greater ability to relate to members of the opposite sex on account of their celibacy. A Theravadin Buddhist monk writes, "It may be interesting to note that many monks have found that after becoming established in the practice of celibacy their ability to relate to women as individuals rather than sexual objects is greatly enhanced. There is a warmth free from the idea of gaining something. We see clearly, in the words of Ajahn Buddhadassa, that we are all 'companions in dukkha.' "[10] The subtle harmonizing of dispassion and empathy evident in this monk's comment is the balance Moggallana and the monk in the Zen koan are lacking.

Returning to Vimala's part in the interaction, it is clear that she has her problems too. In the first two stanzas of her poem, we get a sense of her egoism and anger. On the one hand, Vimala is proud of her sexual power. She has built her identity around it. She says, "I was a hunter and spread my snare for fools...I laughed as I teased them." Yet she hates men, on whom she is at the same time dependent. Given this clash of pride and scorn, Vimala might have felt particularly challenged by Moggallana, not only because of his celibacy, but because of the superior virtue it implied. Though we may recoil from the cruelty of Moggallana's words, they could well have resonated with Vimala's own self-hatred. Vimala's real loathing is not of men but of herself, and she comes nearer to this truth in her poem when she says, "I despised other women."

Having grown up in an ungentle world, Vimala's next step is as interesting as the resolution to the Zen koan is unexpected. She becomes a renunciant. This new step can be viewed from several perspectives. It is possible that renunciation is merely a new form of her old self-hatred, in which Vimala imitates Moggallana's fear and re-jection of her sexuality. From this perspective, the line from her poem "I have cut men and gods out of my life," would be equivalent to Moggallana's rejection of her. On the other hand, in the fourth stanza of her poem, Vimala says, "I, my same self." This detail sug-gests that she has not rejected the person she once was, but instead is affirming a continuity in her life. From this point of view, the line "I have cut men and gods out of my life," instead of implying that she has built an impenetrable wall around herself, shows rather that she is no longer ruled by inside images or outside forces. In this read-ing, Vimala becomes a renunciant who is not afraid of the world, a person who is truly free.

> Young,
> intoxicated by my own
> lovely skin,
> my figure,
> my gorgeous looks,
> and famous too,
> I despised other women.
>
> Dressed to kill
> at the whorehouse door,
> I was a hunter
> and spread my snare for fools.
>
> And when I stripped for them
> I was the woman of their dreams;
> I laughed as I teased them.
>
> Today,
> head shaved,
> robed,
> alms-wanderer,
> I, my same self,
> sit at the tree's foot;
> no thought.[11]

All ties
untied,
I have cut men and gods
out of my life,

I have quenched the fires.

ADDHAKASI

In a previous life, Addhakasi had once reviled a woman renunciant, calling her a prostitute. For this act of wrong speech, she was reborn as a prostitute in the kingdom of Kasi.

In those days, Kasi (today the modern city of Varanasi [Benares]) was a riverport of major significance. The region was famous for its cotton, silk, and many other products. A newly emerging class of wealthy merchants flourished. Prostitutes, in turn, made big money. Addhakasi's name relates to this affluent economy. The revenue of Kasi was one thousand pieces of money per day. Kasi literally meant "one thousand." Addha meant "one half," hence five hundred pieces of money. In her poem, it explicitly says that her fee was "one thousand" pieces of money. Her name can then be explained in two ways. Either she was called Addhakasi because a night with her, half of twenty-four hours, cost her patron half of the daily revenue of Kasi. Or, her fee of one thousand pieces of money was so exorbitant for even her most wealthy patrons, that many visited her for briefer periods at the half price of five hundred.

Apart from its secular activities, Kasi was also a center of Brahmanic culture, as well as a place frequented by a variety of religious teachers. The Buddha came often to Kasi. In fact, it was just outside of Kasi, in the Deer Park at Sarnath, that he delivered his first sermon. Addhakasi did not hear that sermon, but she did hear him preach a later one. On the basis of it, she decided to join the community of nuns. Later on, she sought full ordination. The story, quoted from the *Cullavagga*, is as follows:

> Now at that time a courtesan named Addhakasi had adopted the religious life under the *bhikkhunis,* and she wanted to go to Savatthi to be received as a full member of the sangha by the Blessed One himself. And men of abandoned life heard of

this and beset the road. Addhakasi in turn heard that they had done so, and sent a messenger to the Blessed One saying, "I want to receive the *upasampada* initiation. What course of action should I take?"

[Then the Buddha agreed that the ordination could be conferred by a messenger and the monks sent first a monk, then a female student, then a male novice, then a female novice, then an ignorant, incompetent nun. In each case, the Buddha rejected the ordination, until finally he said,]

"I allow you, O monks, to confer the *upasampada* initiation by sending a learned, competent nun as a messenger."[12]

Addhakasi's ordination thus established a precedent whereby nuns were allowed further religious authority. Her poem, like Vimala's, records her former lifestyle, her conversion, and her realization.

> I used to be priceless.
> When they set my fee
> it was the same
> as all the revenue
> of Kasi.
>
> Then disgust.
> I couldn't care less
> about my beautiful body.
>
> I wish to stop running,
> never to go
> from birth to birth
> again.
>
> The three knowledges have been realized.
> The Buddha's teaching has been done.

PADUMAVATI

Although this woman was referred to as Abhayamata ("the mother of the monk Abhaya") in the *Therigatha*, her own name was Padumavati. Paduma is a lotus, and Padumavati is an Indian goddess, ruler of serpents. Women were frequently named after goddesses.

Renowned for her beauty, Padumavati worked as a prostitute in her native town of Ujjeni, but her reputation extended as far as the palace of King Bimbisara in Magadha. There Bimbisara's curiosity was aroused, and he had his minister conjure a spirit which could carry him to Ujjeni to meet Padumavati. Their affair resulted in a child, and Bimbisara pronounced that if it were a son, the child should be brought to the palace. Thus, when she bore a son and he reached seven years of age, Padumavati sent him to Bimbisara, and he was raised in the royal household.

In the first stanza of Padumavati's poem, her son, having become a Buddhist monk, speaks. He is teaching her the meditation on the thirty-two parts of the body, a meditation commonly given at one's first initiation. In the second stanza, Padumavati announces the realization she has gained through the use of this technique.

[Padumavati's Son:]
> Mother,
> from the hair of the head down,
> and the soles of the feet up
> look at this dirty, stinking body.

[Padumavati:]
> Thinking like this
> rooted out desire.
> The burning fever ended.
> I am quenched.

AMBAPALI

Her origins were supernatural. According to legends, Ambapali came to birth spontaneously in the city of Vesali. She was discovered by a gardener at the foot of a mango tree—her name, Ambapali, means "mango protectress," or "mango guardian." She was so astonishingly beautiful that princes fought to possess her. The strife was settled by appointing her the chief courtesan of Vesali. Because of her, Vesali was said to have become very prosperous.

Among Ambapali's patrons was King Bimbisara. Like Padumavati, Ambapali also bore a son by Bimbisara who became a Buddhist monk. These sons seem to have become convincing proselytizers; Ambapali's son too was influential in his mother's decision to renounce the world.

Ambapali abandoned fame and money to become a devout Buddhist disciple. She had never heard the Buddha preach, though he was by now a man in his late sixties or early seventies, with a wide reputation and following. When Ambapali learned that Gautama was preaching in a nearby town, she went out to meet him and hear his sermon. She also invited him and his monks to eat with her the coming day. Gautama accepted, and though later that day he received a similar invitation from the powerful and prestigious Licchavis tribe, he postponed that lunch until the day after his lunch with Ambapali, in order to keep his promise to her.

When the next day dawned, the Buddha warned his monks to guard their passion and to be careful not to lose their heads over Ambapali. From Ambapali's point of view, the event was a great success. As a result, she built a hermitage on her land and gave it to the sangha. It was in that very place that the Buddha rested in his eightieth year, four months before he died.

Ambapali's poem, while not a formal meditation—as, for instance, the meditation on the thirty-two parts of the body—similarly seeks to bring the image of impermanence into focus. In this respect it is a serious poem. But it also strikes us, and probably struck the ancient Indians as well, as humorous. For this reason, it is the only poem in this collection which has been translated into rhyme, as rhyme seems befitting of its humor.

It is interesting to note the striking parallels between Ambapali's poem and another ancient love poem, the bridegroom's poem in the *Song of Songs*. Both compare the beauty of a woman to the most resplendent things in nature. But whereas the bridegroom, King Solomon, in the *Old Testament* poem can see only the beauty, Ambapali's poem emphasizes the contrast between former beauty and the ugliness of old age. Here is an excerpt from the *Song of Songs*:

> How beautiful you are, my love,
> how beautiful you are!

Your eyes behind your veil
are doves;
your hair is like a flock of goats
frisking down the slopes of Gilead.
Your teeth are like a flock of shorn ewes
as they come up from the washing.
Each one has its twin,
not one unpaired with another.
Your lips are a scarlet thread
and your words enchanting.
Your cheeks, behind your veil,
are halves of pomegranate.
Your neck is the tower of David
built as a fortress,
hung round with a thousand bucklers,
and each the shield of a hero.
Your two breasts are two fawns,
twins of a gazelle,
that feed among the lilies.[13]

While the bridegroom's song strikes us as lovely, Ambapali's poem evokes a mixture of humor and disgust. That Ambapali's poem succeeds so well in evoking disgust means that it has achieved its purpose. Such poetry was first and last religious, not aesthetic. Here the purpose was to jolt the listener into anxiety about her or his own transiency, hopefully stimulating in that person the desire to renounce the world and strive for enlightenment.

My hair was black and curly
the color of black bees.
Now that I am old
it is like the hemp of trees.
This is the teaching of one who speaks truth.

Fragrant as a scented oak
I wore flowers in my hair.
Now because of old age,

it smells like dog's hair.
This is the teaching of one who speaks truth.

It was thick as a grove
and I parted it with comb and pin.
Now because of old age,
it is thin, very thin.
This is the teaching of one who speaks truth.

I had fine braids
fastened with gold.
Now old age
has made me bald.
This is the teaching of one who speaks truth.

My eyebrows were crescents,
painted well.
Now they droop, and
are wrinkled as well.
This is the teaching of one who speaks truth.

My eyes flashed like jewels,
long, black.
Now they don't make
anyone look back.
This is the teaching of one who speaks truth.

My earlobes were beautiful
as bracelets, highly-crafted and bright.
Now they sag
and have wrinkles alright.
This is the teaching of one who speaks truth.

My teeth were beautiful
the color of plantain buds.
Now because of old age
they are broken and yellow.
This is the teaching of one who speaks truth.

I had a sweet voice
like a cuckoo moving in a thicket.
Now cracked and halting
you can hear my age in it.
This is the teaching of one who speaks truth.

My neck was beautiful
like a polished conch shell.
Now because of old age
it bends and bows.
This is the teaching of one who speaks truth.

My arms were beautiful
twin pillars, they hung free.
Now because of old age,
they are weak as the patali tree.
This is the teaching of one who speaks truth.

My hands were beautiful
set off by rings gold as the sun.
Now because of old age
they are radishes or onions.
This is the teaching of one who speaks truth.

My breasts were beautiful
high, close together and round.
Now like empty water bags,
they hang down.
This is the teaching of one who speaks truth.

My thighs were beautiful
like an elephant's trunk.
Now because of old age
They are like bamboo stalks.
This is the teaching of one who speaks truth.

My calves were beautiful
gold anklets I wore as jewelry,

Now these same calves
look like sticks of sesame.
This is the teaching of one who speaks truth.

My feet were beautiful
delicate as if filled with cotton.
Now because of old age
they are cracked and rotten.
This is the teaching of one who speaks truth.

This is how my body was.
Now it is dilapidated,
the place of pain,
an old house
with the plaster falling off.

ANOPAMA

Anopama was the daughter of a financier named Majjha, a member
of the new merchant class that was rising to prominence during the
sixth century B.C.E.. Her father's wealth, in common with this new
class, was measured in money rather than in cattle (as had formerly
been the case in previous centuries). Wealth was becoming private
property in the sense that it was at his own disposal instead of being
tied up by clan or tribal obligations.

Anopama means "without equal." Because her beauty was extraordinary, the Therigatha Commentary points out an association between her name and her beauty. But it is also possible that this name
was given to her by her parents, not because of her physical beauty,
but on account of qualities that were more intangible. One is re-
minded of the story of King Pasenadi's disappointment on learning
of the birth of a daughter instead of a son. In a culture where the
birth of sons was desired, the Buddha's comment that a girl "may
prove even a better offspring" than a boy,[14] implies the idea of no
comparison, or "without equal." In this sense, the name Anopama
may suggest not beauty, but uniqueness.

I was born into a family
great in property and wealth,
Majjha's daughter.
My skin and figure were lovely.

Sons of kings sought me out.
Sons of merchants longed for me.

There was one who sent
my father a messenger.
"Give me Anopama
and I will give you
eight times her weight
in gold and jewels."

But I have seen the Enlightened One,
first in the world, unsurpassed,
and I bowed at his feet
and sat down to one side.

In his compassion, Gautama taught me.
Sitting right here
I gained the third fruit of meditation.[15]
Then I cut off my hair
and turned toward homelessness.
This is the seventh night
since my craving has died.

ABHIRUPA-NANDA

Abhirupa-Nanda was born into a Sakyan family in Kapilavatthu. Because Nanda was a common name, like our Mary or Jane, her story has become intertwined with those of several other nuns named Nanda, including a Janapadakalyni-Nanda, and Pajapati's daughter, Sundari-Nanda.

Abhirupa-Nanda was the daughter of a man named Khema and his chief wife. When Abhirupa-Nanda came of age, the day arrived when she was to choose her husband from among a number of suitors. For some unexpected reason, the man of her choice, Carabhuta, died that very day. Though she had had the freedom to make her own choice, she was not given that privilege twice. Perhaps the suitor's death was considered a bad sign. In any case, against her will, her parents made her leave the world.

Abhirupa-Nanda wanted to be married; she didn't want to be a nun. As might be expected, she put up resistance. One day Gautama requested Pajapti to bring the nuns before him to receive instruction. Abhirupa-Nanda refused to show up and sent a proxy instead. The Buddha said, "Let no one come by proxy." So she was compelled to appear in person. As he had done before, Gautama created before Abhirupa-Nanda an image of a woman as beautiful as she, and made the apparition age before her eyes. The point struck home, and from that time on Abhirupa-Nanda practiced with great diligence.

Abhirupa-Nanda's poem has the same first two lines as Sundari-Nanda's poem from Chapter One. In the first stanza of Abhirupa-Nanda's poem is a reference to one of two possible meditation practices: the contemplation of the corpse in nine stages of decay, or, as in Padumavati's poem, contemplation of the thirty-two parts of the body. Because nuns were forbidden to meditate in cemeteries, it is more likely that Abhirupa-Nanda practiced the latter meditation. The instruction is for the devotee to meditate on the fact that the body, from head to foot, is full of impurities. The way to take up this theme, discussed in the *Visuddhimagga*,[16] is to repeat the list of the parts of the body hundreds or thousands of times, aloud or to oneself, thereby inducing concentration. To this day in Theravadin Buddhist countries, this is a standard meditation practice assigned to the newly ordained.

In the second stanza, Abhirupa-Nanda is exhorted to meditate on the unconditioned. What is this? Buddhism speaks of the "marks of existence." These are anything born from a cause and therefore subject to decay, in other words subject to karma's endless round of cause and effect, birth and death. The three marks are greed, hatred and ignorance. The unconditioned is that which is free of the three marks. The middle line of the second stanza speaks of using all possible means to get rid of the tendency to judge oneself. This is another frequent injunction.

Nanda,
look at the body,
diseased, impure, rotten.
Focus the mind
on all this foulness.

Meditate on the unconditioned.
Get rid of the tendency
to judge yourself
above, below, or
equal to others.
By penetrating deeply
into judgment
you will live at peace.

JENTI

Jenti came from Vesali, the same town as Vimala and Ambapali. She
was a member of the Licchavis tribe. Like Abhirupa-Nanda, she was
considered beautiful and conceited. But as a nun, she attained the
seven qualities of enlightenment—concentration, energy, rapture,
investigation, tranquility, equanimity, and mindfulness. Jenti's second stanza is not her individual utterance but is from the oral
tradition's common stock of verse. The same stanza is found in
Mahapajapati's poem.

The Buddha taught
seven qualities of enlightenment.
They are ways to find peace
and I have developed them all.

For I have seen the Blessed One.
This is my last body,
and I will not go
from birth to birth again.
This is my last rebirth.

[1] H.T. Francis and E.J. Thomas. *Jataka Tales*. (Cambridge: Cambridge University Press, 1916), p. 352.

[2] E.W. Burlingame. *Buddhaghosa's "Dhammapada" Commentary (Dhammapadatthakatha)*. 3 Vols. Harvard Oriental Series, Vol. 28 (Cambridge: Harvard University Press, 1921), p. 311.

[3] Nancy Falk. "An Image of Women in Old Buddhist Literature" in *Women and Religion*. Judith Plaskow and Joan Arnold, ed. (Missoula, Montana: Scholars Press, 1974), p. 110.

[4] Katherine Marsh. *The Theriigatha and Theraagatha*. Mimeographed thesis. Cornell University, 1980, p. 10.

[5] I.B. Horner, tr. *The Book of Discipline (Suttavibhanga)*. Vol. III. (London: Oxford University Press Warehouse, 1942), p. 247. I have altered Horner's translation slightly to make it read more smoothly.

[6] *Ibid.*, p. 283. Again, I have altered Horner's translation slightly.

[7] K.R. Norman, tr. *The Elders Verses II. Theragatha*. (London: Luzac and Co. Ltd., 1966), p. 106.

[8] *Samyutta Nikaya* 41, 14.

[9] David Meltzer, ed. *Birth: An Anthology of Ancient Texts, Songs, Prayers and Stories*. (Berkeley: North Point Press, 1980)

[10] Wat Pah Nanachat to Susan Murcott, personal letter. August, 1978. "We are all 'companions in *dukkha*.' "—*dukkha* is the Pali word for "suffering."

[11] *avitakka*, lit. "free from conceptual thinking." The meditator achieves this degree of concentration and realization in the second *jhana*.

[12] Max Müller, ed. *Vinaya: Kullavagga*. translated by T.W. Rhys Davids and Hermann Oldenberg. *Sacred Books of the East*, Vol. 20. (Oxford: Clarendon Press, 1885. Rep. by Delhi: Motilal Banarsidass, 1969), p. 360.

[13] *The Jerusalem Bible*. (New York: Doubleday and Company, Inc., 1966)

[14] *Samyutta Nikaya* iii, 2,6.

[15] *Tatiyan phalam*, lit. "the third fruit." This denotes that the nun has attained the third stage of holiness, the fourth of which constitutes arahantship.

[16] Caroline Rhys Davids. *The Visuddhi-Magga of Buddhaghosa*. Vol I. (London: pub. for the Pali Text Society by Oxford University Press, 1920), p. 178ff.

CHAPTER NINE

Friends & Sisters

We have seen a number of examples in the preceding chapters of family playing a crucial role in a woman's decision to join the order of nuns. Bhadda shared with her husband an equal desire to become a renunciant, and together they put on robes and shaved their heads; Dhammadinna and Capa followed in their husbands' footsteps by becoming nuns; Pajapati's daughter, Sundari-Nanda, joined the order because all her kin had done so; Mutta joined to escape from the three crooked things, one of which was her husband; Sundari, like her father, became ordained because of grief over the death of her brother. These are but a few examples which show the influence of family in motivating a woman to become a nun.

Not only did a woman's family play a large role in effecting her decision to become a nun, but her friends also could be a major force. The term *mitta* ("friend") is used with several different meanings in the Buddhist Canon. We could say that these various meanings are tied to the three treasures of Buddhism—Buddha, Dharma, and Sangha. In the *Mahavagga*, the Buddha describes himself as the "Good Friend" and counsels his disciples to understand that friendship with "the good," that is, with the Buddha's teaching, is the complete holy life.[1] The Buddha is the quintessential "Good Friend" in the sense of being the one who leads others to "friendship" with the Dharma. These are two ways the term "friend" or "friendship" is used. In this chapter, friendship is meant in the more ordinary sense of the word: the deep liking and appreciation of one for another. In this respect, friendship has an affinity with the third treasure, Sangha. It was on account of a special friendship that various women joined the community of nuns.

It is very touching that the theme of friendship should appear and reappear in the *Therigatha*. Two nuns have the name "Mitta". The nun Kisagotami praises friendship in the opening lines of her poem:

> With good friends
> even a fool can be wise.
> Keep good company

and wisdom grows.
Those who keep good company
can be freed from suffering.

Nuns especially had the opportunity to develop deep friendships. It was an offense for a nun not to "leave at hand's reach a nun who is a companion." This rule, intended for the protection of the nuns, meant constant association and interaction. The women's physical proximity could sometimes be the occasion for intimate friendships. In light of the importance of friendship, the Buddha devotes an entire discourse to this theme, teaching that:

> One who says, "I am your friend" but does not take upon herself any tasks she is capable of doing, is to be recognized as no friend. But she on whom one can rely, like a child sleeping on its mother's breast, is truly a friend who cannot be parted from one by others.[2]

Friendship is a marvelous gift with its capacity to free a person from suffering, to establish a trust as deep as a child's trust for its mother. In this chapter we meet women who are such friends: Sama, the companion of Samavati, who renounces the world at the death of her friend; Abhaya, childhood friend of the prostitute Padumavati; Vijaya, friend of the brilliant and beautiful Khema. In each case their friendship led them to the Buddhist teaching, and hence, freed them from suffering. Then we have the poems of three women who were biological sisters—Cala, Upacala, and Sisupacala. These are the only women in the *Therigatha* known to have been related in this way.

SAMA

Sama came from Kosambi. One of the things she valued most in her life was the love of her friend, Samavati, who was known for her devotion to the Buddhist path and for her kindness. But Samavati died tragically and, in her grief, Sama chose to renounce the world, becoming a Buddhist nun.

Actually, there are two women in the *Therigatha* with the name Sama, and there is some confusion as to their identities. Both were from Kosambi, both were said to have been friends of Samavati, both supposedly joined the community of nuns in grief over the death of their friend. To add still one more layer of confusion, Samavati's name can also be shortened to Sama. It is possible that there really were two different women who came from Kosambi, who were friends of Samavati, who became nuns, and who composed two very similar poems. But it seems more likely that the two poems attributed to two different women named Sama are two different versions of one poem, and that we are actually talking about one woman. Nothing more is known about the nun(s) Sama.

If the company a person keeps reflects something of her own character, then knowing more about Samavati is a way to learn a little more about Sama. Samavati was a prominent laywoman of the early Buddhist community. She came from a merchant's family of Bhaddavati. When plague broke out there, the family fled to Kosambi, but within a matter of days, her parents developed the symptoms of the disease and died. Samavati was adopted by Ghosaka, a family friend who was treasurer to King Udena.

Samavati grew to become a beautiful young woman. One day Udena, whose kingdom was all of Kosambi (located about one hundred miles south and east of Pasenadi's kingdom of Kosala), met Samavati, fell in love with her, and asked his subject Ghosaka to give her to him. Ghosaka refused. In retaliation, Udena had Ghosaka and his wife turned out of their home. Concerned for their plight, Samavati made the decision to go to Udena and become one of his chief consorts. In addition to her, Udena had two other consorts, Magandiya and Vasuladatta. He would spend a week at a time with each.

Samavati's rival, Magandiya, had originally been offered to Siddhartha Gautama, when he was visiting Kosambi in his ninth rainy season as a religious teacher. But the Buddha, by then well established in his renunciation and life work, refused, calling Magandiya a "corpse, a bag of filth."[3] It was after this that Magandiya was given to Udena. Based on her particular experience, she may well have had legitimate doubts about the authenticity of this renunciant Gautama's compassion, at least as far as it concerned her or perhaps women in general.

Samavati, on the other hand, had an entirely different perspective on the Buddha. She first learned of his teachings through her slave woman, Khujjuttara. Samavati used to regularly give eight coins to Khujjuttara, four of which were to be used for flowers to decorate her home, and four of which were for Khujjuttara to keep. When, one day, Samavati found the house overflowing with flowers, she asked why. It turned out that Khujjuttara had spent all her money that day on flowers, out of joy in hearing, for the first time, the Buddha preach. Khujjuttara then preached to Samavati and all her women attendants, and every single one was converted. They begged Khujjuttara to be their teacher, to go to the discourses the Buddha gave, and return and teach them. Because Khujjuttara, as a slave, had greater freedom of mobility than the more confined upper-class woman, she could do this. So Khujjuttara went, and became renowned for knowing the *Tipitaka*, the Buddhist canon, by heart, and for her ability to preach the Dharma. Through her, Samavati became a devout disciple.

We can imagine that the devotion Samavati showed to the Buddha's teachings would not have endeared her to Magandiya. This tension would have been in addition to the strain of being co-wives (a verse from Kisagotami's poem comes to mind: "How hard it is to be a woman. / It is hard to be one wife among others...") When Magandiya could bear it no longer, she framed a conspiracy in which Samavati would be accused of an attempted assassination of Udena. This backfired, and by way of apology, Udena granted Samavati a special favor, whatever she desired. Samavati asked Udena to allow the Buddha to come each day to the palace and preach to her and her attendants. This must have enraged Magandiya all the more. In this state, Magandiya set fire to a house inside of which Samavati and her companions were locked. No one escaped. Afterwards, the Buddha acknowledged that these deceased women had attained important levels of realization, some the first, others the second, and still others the third stage of the path of realization.

It was after these events that Sama, in sorrow, renounced the world. For twenty-five years, her mind was always distracted while in meditation, but finally Sama attained the fourth and highest stage of the path, becoming an *arahant*.

Following is one of the two similar poems attributed to a nun named Sama.

> It was twenty-five years
> since I turned away from home
> and I hadn't had a moment's peace.
>
> I had no peace
> because I didn't know my own mind.
>
> Then suddenly I was shaken with dread,
> remembering the words
> of the conqueror.[4]
>
> Because
> of the pain of things
> I love to be alert.
>
> I have finished with craving.
> The Buddha's teaching has been done.
> It is the seventh day
> since my craving died.

Abhaya

Abhaya was a childhood friend of Padumavati (see Chapter Eight). Both women grew up in Ujjeni, and must have been very dear friends, as Abhaya followed Padumavati in joining the order of nuns.

Abhaya's name means "without fear." In the Pali Canon and the Upanishads, a person who has realized the highest truth is referred to by the epithet *abhaya*. It is an appropriate name for this nun, as she is the only one among the nuns whose enlightenment occurs while contemplating either a corpse or the remains of a corpse. This detail is alluded to in her poem and is mentioned in the *Therigatha* Commentary. The precise practice, described in the *Visuddhimagga*, is called a "Buddhist Meditation on the Tenfold Foulness of the Corpses." Some of these ten foulnesses include:

...the swollen corpse, as demonstrating the downfall of the
shape of the body...beneficial for one who lusts after beautiful
shapes; the bluish corpse, as demonstrating the ruin of the
color of the skin...beneficial for one who lusts after the beauty
of the skin; the gnawed corpse, as demonstrating the destruction of the once proud outlines of the protrusions of the flesh,
is beneficial for one who lusts after the protrusions of the flesh,
at the breasts or in similar parts of the body; the worm-eaten
corpse, by demonstrating that the body belongs in common to
manifold kinds of worms...beneficial for one who lusts after his
body with the thought, "this is mine."

After going through the complete list of ten, the meditation
instruction continues:

Therefore, as regards its unclean, evil-smelling, loathsome and
repulsive condition, there is no difference between the body
of a king and that of an outcast. When, with the help of tooth-
picks, by washing the face,...when one has covered up the private parts with various garments, when one has anointed the
body with sweet-smelling ointments of the most various col-
ors, when one has adorned it with flowers, ornaments, and
suchlike, then one manages to give it an appearance which
makes it possible to seize upon it as 'I and mine.' Hence it is
because they do not perceive the mark of abominableness,
which characterizes the true and proper nature of the body, but
is concealed for them by the adventitious adornments, that
men take delight in women, and women in men. But in reality there is in the body not even the tiniest spot that would be
worth regarding as delightful.[5]

Such a meditation surely was for one "without fear."

It was a rule of the Order that nuns, unlike monks, were not allowed to meditate in burial grounds. Abhaya's meditation and enlightenment might have taken place before this rule existed. She
may have stretched the rule to meet her need. Or she may have
meditated on images of bones or corpses which, though not in burial
grounds, were sights of everyday experience.

Abhaya,
this body,

that ordinary people cling to
is so fragile.

With full attention,
completely aware,
I will throw this body down.

Because
of the pain of things
I love to be watchful.

I have finished with craving.
The Buddha's teaching has been done.

VIJAYA

Vijaya was a very dear friend of Khema, who was considered to have
had the clearest insight (see Chapter Three). Born in Rajagaha,
Bimbisara's capital city, Vijaya was from a humble background.
Khema, by contrast, had grown up in luxury. Yet the bond between
them was so strong that when Khema decided to become a nun,
Vijaya, having listened to Khema's teaching, came to the same
resolve. And like Khema, Vijaya was naturally gifted and swiftly
realized the highest truth.

Vijaya was one among the nuns whom Mara attempted to seduce
by taking the form of a beautiful young man. He told her that she
was young and attractive, that he was too, and that they should enjoy each other. Vijaya's reply was in keeping with her discipline. She
said, "I delight in observing emptiness, the unreality of the body, and
don't desire your soft touches. My ignorance is dispelled." Mara, having no power over her, went away.[6]

In the fifth stanza, Vijaya's religious experience is expressed in the
formulaic style of the Buddha's enlightenment verses. Her insight
deepens during three stages of the night, from the first watch (the
hours from 6 p.m. to 10 p.m.), through the middle watch (10 p.m.
to 2 a.m.), to the last watch of the night (2 a.m. to 6 a.m.).

Four or five times
I left my cell.

I had no peace of mind,
no control over mind.

I went to a nun
and respectfully
asked her questions.

She taught me the Dharma,
earth, water, fire and air,
the nature of perception,
the Four Noble Truths,
the faculties, the powers,
the seven qualities of enlightenment,
and the eightfold way
to the highest goal.

When I heard her words
I followed her advice.

In the first watch of the night,
I remembered I had been born before.
In the middle watch of the night,
the eye of heaven became clear.
In the last watch of the night
I tore apart
the great dark.

Then I lived
with joy and happiness
filling my whole body
and after seven days
I stretched out my feet
having torn apart
the great dark.

CALA, UPACALA, AND SISUPACALA

Cala, Upacala, and Sisupacala were biological sisters. Cala was the
eldest, Upacala the middle, and Sisupacala the youngest sister. Their

older brother was Sariputta, the great monk. All were children of the brahman Surupasari, and lived in Magadha in the village of Nalaka. When Sariputta joined the Buddha's order, his sisters, in admiration, said, "If Sariputta follows this path, it is no ordinary way," and the three decided to become Buddhist renunciants as well. Though we know no further details about their lives, we can glimpse something of their character and relationship in the similarity of their poems. Not only are all three poems dialogues with Mara, the last three stanzas in each are practically identical.

In each of the poems, Mara is the evil antagonist. Having already met this figure, Mara, in a number of *Therigatha* poems, a few words about him are in order. Mara dominates Pali Buddhist demonology. Mara literally means "death." He is the embodiment of death and temptation, especially the temptations of passion and evil. Sometimes the term "mara" is applied to the whole of worldly existence, the world of rebirth, as opposed to *nirvana*. Mara is frequently personified as a single male figure, though he is sometimes accompanied by his armies or his three seductive daughters. He has the power, in common with other *yakkhas* and spirits of the Buddhist mythological pantheon, to change shape at will as a part of his efforts to seduce or destroy. In the *Mahavastu* he is called the "great *yakkha*," the great spirit.[7]

Mara does not appear in earlier Hindu mythology. In fact, "no conception equivalent to Mara is to be found in Indian mythology."[8] The Mara legend is closely connected with the Buddha. The Buddha overcame Mara—death and *samsara*—by his enlightenment. Henceforth, for the Buddha, like other enlightened *arahants*, there would be no more rebirths. A poetical stock phrase is used to proclaim this fact, a phrase repeated in the poems of the three sisters, and occurring also in the poems of Uppalavanna, Soma, Sela, and others; "And Death / you too are destroyed." The phrase is indicative, not of conflict, but of dismissal. The enlightened ones are entirely unassailable by Mara, because they have the power simply to ignore him. To do so is to dismiss him. A common stock phrase is voiced by Mara when he has been foiled: "*Janati mam Bhagava, janati mam Sugato!*" "*The Lord knows me! The Righteous One knows me!*" In the following dialogue poems, Mara's role is to tempt, to confuse, to seduce, to lead astray.

An aspect of Cala's poem also deserves special attention. In the third and fourth stanzas, the notion of "views" is mentioned: "All those outside the way depend on views... He taught me the way— the complete overcoming of views." A view, *ditthi*, is a belief, dogma, theory, religious teaching or ideology. On one level, there are "right" and "wrong" views (*ditthi-ppata* and *miccha-ditthi*). Clearly, the Buddhist disciple wants to choose the "right" view, the teachings of the Buddha. But on a subtler level, she or he wants to completely overcome views. This is what Cala describes in the fourth stanza; it is what is meant in the famous Zen Buddhist *koan*, "When you meet the Buddha, kill the Buddha"; and again by Gautama's purported dying words, "Be a lamp unto yourself." The idea is one of non-attachment to any fixed belief, even belief in the Buddha himself! This is a highly iconoclastic notion, but one suited to a renunciant tradition such as early Buddhism.

Some scholars feel that "overcoming all views" is the Buddha's earliest teaching. The four *atthakas* (octets) of the *Atthakavagga*, arguably the oldest strata of the *Pali Canon*, do not mention what we consider basic doctrines of early Buddhism (*nirvana*, *samsara*, the *skandhas*, etc.), but instead lay particular emphasis on the importance of overcoming all views. In his essay "The Octets of the *Atthakavagga*" Nelson Foster writes,

> For the Gautama of the *atthakas* to be bound to even one view was to fall headlong into the trap of accepting and rejecting. Gautama's preponderant attention in the *atthakas* to views, as opposed to pleasures, [makes it] legitimate to conclude that later Buddhism distorted the original teaching, expanding and warping Gautama's stand on pleasures to make it serve new purposes and underplaying the profundity of "no views."[9]

Though this statement is provocative, there is abundant evidence to support the position that the Buddha originally taught the danger of sense pleasures, as well as the concept of "no views." But Foster's point, drawn from the evidence of the earliest strata of the *Pali Canon*, underscores the respect for the notion of "no views" by the earliest community of believers. That the idea of "no views" might have been later overshadowed relative to cutting out craving and passion was probably only natural in a celibate community.

Whether "no views" is an original teaching or not, it is the central message of Cala's poem. In Upacala's poem the concern is with sensual pleasure and the cycle of birth and rebirth, and Sisupacala's poem emphasizes the theme of birth and death.

CALA

[Cala:]

> I, a nun, trained and self-composed,
> established mindfulness
> and entered peace like an arrow.
> The elements of body and mind grew still,
> happiness came.

[Mara:]

> Who told you to shave your head?
> You look like a renunciant to me—
> why do you practice this nonsense?

[Cala:]

> All those outside the Way
> depend on views.
> They don't know the Dharma.
> They have no real understanding.
>
> But in the Sakya clan
> the unrivaled Buddha was born.
> He taught me the Way—
> the complete overcoming of views:
>
> pain,
> the cause of pain,
> the end of pain,
> and the great Eightfold Way
> that stills all pain.
>
> When I heard his words
> I rejoiced.

The three knowledges have been realized.
The Buddha's teaching has been done.

Everywhere the love of pleasure is destroyed,
the great dark is torn apart,
and Death,
you too are destroyed.

UPACALA

[Upacala:]

I was a nun
mindful, clear-sighted, and self-composed.
There is a peace that evil does not know
and I entered peace like an arrow.

[Mara:]

What's wrong with being born?
From that, we have the pleasures of the flesh.
Take your delight while you can—
if you don't, you'll regret it.

[Upacala:]

We are born into death—
the severing of hands and feet,
slaughter, bonds, and torment;
we are born into pain.

But someone who cannot be conquered
was born in the Sakya clan.
He is enlightened.
He taught me the Way—
how to overcome birth completely:

pain,
the cause of pain,
the end of pain,
and the great Eightfold Way
that stills all pain.

When I heard his words
I rejoiced.

The three knowledges have been realized.
The Buddha's teaching has been done.

Everywhere the love of pleasure is destroyed,
the great dark is torn apart,
and Death,
you too are destroyed.

SISUPACALA

[Sisupacala:]
    A nun who has self-possession
and integrity
will find the peace that nourishes
and never causes surfeit.

[Mara:]
    The deities of the Heaven of the Thirty-Three[10]
where Indra rules,
the deities who are free from misery,
the deities who have attained bliss,
the happy creators who make their own pleasure,
and the deities who control what others create;
turn your mind to those places
where you lived before.

[Sisupacala:]
    Time after time,
from life to life,
the deities of the Heaven of the Thirty-Three
where Indra rules,
the deities who are free from misery,
the deities who have attained bliss,
the happy creators who make their own pleasure,
and the deities who control what others create,
lead individual lives,

but cannot free themselves,
chasing after birth and death.

The whole world is burning.
The whole world is in flames.
The whole world is blazing.
The whole world shakes.

But the Buddha taught me the unshakable Way.
Ordinary people don't practice it,
and there is nothing to which you can compare it.

When I heard his words
I lived in the joy of the teaching.

The three knowledges have been realized.
The Buddha's teaching has been done.

Everywhere the love of pleasure is destroyed,
the great dark is torn apart,
and Death,
you too are destroyed.

---

[1] John Ireland, ed. *Samyutta Nikaya* V., *Mahavagga* XLV. (Kandy, Sri Lanka: Buddhist Publication Society, 1967), p. 75.

[2] V. Fausboll, ed. *Suttanipata*. 2 Vols. (London, Henry Frowde, 1885-1894), vv. 253-255.

[3] E.W. Burlingame, tr. *Buddhaghosa's Dhammapada Commentary (Dhammapadatthakatha)*. 3 Vols. Harvard Oriental Series, Vol. 28. (Cambridge: Harvard University Press, 1921), p. 34.

[4] This is an epithet of the Buddha.

[5] Caroline Rhys Davids, ed. *The Visuddhi-Magga of Buddhaghosa*. 2 Vols. (London: Oxford University Press, 1920-1921), pp. 178ff.

[6] Bimala Churn Law, "Buddhist Women," in *Indian Antiquary*. (May-March 1928), p. 53.

[7] *"Mahantam yaksam,"* Mahavastu. ii 260; 261. II

[8] T.O. Ling. *Buddhism and the Mythology of Evil.* (London: Geo. Allen and Unwin Ltd., 1962), p. 46.

[9] Nelson Foster. "The Octets of the Atthakavagga." Unpublished essay. (University of Hawaii, 1979), p. 7.

[10] These are the *devas* of the five heavenly realms: the *Tavatimsa*, *Yama*, *Tusita*, *Nimmanarati*, and *Vasavatti devas*. The word *deva* is related to the Latin *deus*; they are "radiant ones," usually invisible to the human eye, but just as subject as humans to the ever-repeating cycle of birth and death. There are many classifications and grades of *devas* and their heavens. This poem makes use of one such classification system, which is common in Buddhist literature.

CHAPTER TEN

Buddhist Nuns & Nature

The stories and poems of this chapter address two aspects of nature—trees, and the moon. The poems are not celebrations of nature, because, with few exceptions, the nuns did not live as hermits away from civilization, but in close association with one another near villages. In this respect their poems differ from those of their male counterparts, the monks of the *Theragatha*, whose poems frequently celebrate some element or creature of the natural world such as wind, rain, mountain, ape, bamboo thicket, or peacock.

Instead, in those nuns' stories or poems where nature is evoked or where the nun is associated with a tree or the moon, there is often a mythic overtone. It is not merely a story or poem about a certain tree or about the moon; a supernatural element comes into play.

NUNS AND TREES

In the stories and poems presented so far, there has occasionally been an association of a particular nun with a tree, grove, or forest. Vimala and Sumangala's mother both go to the foot of a tree to meditate; Dantika goes to the forest. Siha, in her despair, attempts to hang herself from a tree. Subha is taking a walk in the Jivakamba Woods when a man stops her. Uppalavanna lives alone as a hermit in the woods, and, in dialogue with Mara, she is called "a child, standing alone at the foot of the flowering tree." Like Uppalavanna, the three sisters Cala, Upacala, and Sisupacala encounter Mara while in a grove. The sisters have all gone to the Dark Grove after their midday meal to rest under a tree.

In all these examples, while the tree or forest may have significance, it is not magical or deified. This chapter brings together three additional examples which show some kind of association between a nun and a tree. For Soma, not unlike previous examples, the tree is simply an excellent place under which to sit and meditate. But the tree is still a tree, albeit perhaps a special tree. In the second selection we have a nun, Sela, venerating a tree. Here the tree has special powers—or is it that the Buddha and his representative have special powers? Either way, the result is magical. The third example, from the story and poem of Sukka, takes this magic one step further. In this selection, the tree is in fact a deity.

Tree-spirits can be conceptualized in several ways. A tree-spirit can be one with the tree—can animate, live, suffer, and die with the tree, or it can simply use the tree as an abode, from which it comes and goes as it pleases. The tree spirit in Sukka's poem is an example of the latter. A similar tree-spirit is the leading character in a wonderful story from the *Dhammapada*. Here the tree-spirit is a goddess who has a body independent of her tree, but who nevertheless needs a tree of her own as a place to live in. The entire *Dhammapada* story is given below because it helps fill out the picture of how a tree-spirit was conceptualized in ancient Indian folk religion.

After the Teacher had given permission to the Congregation of Monks to lodge outside the walls of the monastery...a certain monk decided to build himself a lodging, and seeing a tree that suited him, began to cut it down. Thereupon a certain spirit who had been reborn in that tree, and who had an infant child, appeared before the monk, carrying her child on her hip, and begged him not to cut down the tree, saying, "Master, do not cut down my home." But the monk said, "I shall not be able to find another tree like this," and paid no further attention to what she said.

The tree-spirit thought to herself, "If he but look upon this child, he will desist," and placed the child on a branch of the tree. The monk, however, had already swung his axe, was unable to check the force of his upraised axe, and cut off the arm of the child. Furious with anger, the tree-spirit raised both her hands and exclaimed, "I will strike him dead." In an instant, however, the thought came to her, "This monk is a righteous man; if I kill him, I shall go to Hell. Moreover, if other tree-spirits see monks cutting down their own trees, they will say to themselves, 'Such and such a tree-spirit killed a monk under such circumstances,' and will follow my example and kill other monks. Besides, this monk has a master; I will therefore content myself with reporting this matter to his master."

Lowering her upraised hands, she went weeping to the Teacher, and having saluted him, stood on one side. Said the Teacher, "What is the matter, tree-spirit?" The tree-spirit replied, "Reverend Sir, your disciple did this and that to me.

I was sorely tempted to kill him, but I thought this and that, refrained from killing him, and came here." So saying, she told him the story in all its details. When the Teacher heard her story, he said to her, "Well done, well done, spirit! You have done well in holding in, like a swift-speeding chariot, your anger when it was thus aroused." So saying, he pronounced the following stanza,

Whoever controls his anger like a swift-speeding chariot, when it is aroused,—
Him I call a charioteer; other folk are merely holders of reins.

At the conclusion of the lesson, the tree-spirit was established in the Fruit of Conversion; the assembled company also profited by it.

But even after the tree-spirit had obtained the Fruit of Conversion, she stood weeping. The Teacher asked her, "What is the matter, tree-spirit?" "Reverend Sir," she replied, "my home has been destroyed; what am I to do now?" Said the Teacher, "Enough, tree-spirit, be not disturbed; I will give you a place of abode." With these words he pointed out near the Perfumed Chamber at Jetavana a certain tree from which a tree-spirit had departed on the preceding day and said, "In such and such a place is a tree which stands by itself; enter therein." Accordingly the tree-spirit entered into that tree. Thenceforth, because the tree-spirit had received her place of abode as a gift from the Buddha, although spirits of great power approached that tree, they were unable to shake it. The Teacher took this occasion to lay down and enjoin upon the monks observance of the precept regarding the injuring of plants and trees.[1]

In this chapter, a tree can be an ordinary tree, a magical tree, a tree-deity dependent on a physical tree for existence, or an independent, anthropomorphized tree-spirit. As a tree-spirit gained the ability to move about independent of a physical tree, it became associated with particular human or divine beings, and certain trees increasingly became symbols of certain deities. Such a person, goddess, or god could then be considered to have gained power over the natural world—For example, the power to make trees bloom, rain fall, sun shine, crops grow, herds and flocks multiply, women conceive, et cetera.

Examples of tree/deity or tree/human associations are abundant in Indus, Vedic-Brahmanic, and Indian folk religion. Relics from Harappa and Mohenjodaro include a naked female figurine with a plant issuing from her womb, and another similar figurine with a lotus coming from her neck. One seal shows a deity in the branches of the sacred fig or pipal tree. (This tree is the *assattha* or *Ficus religiosa*, in Buddhism known as the Bodhi or Bo tree.) While the first two relics associate a plant with a goddess, the third is an obvious case of ancient tree-worship.[2] All these examples from the Indus civilization which associate a plant or tree with a deity suggest a fertility motif.

In a hymn from the *Rig Veda*, a traveller begs a female spirit of the forest (mentioned nowhere else in the *Rig Veda*) not to harm him:

> Spirit of the forest, spirit of the forest, who seems to melt away. How is it that you do not ask where a village is? Doesn't a kind of fear grasp you?
>
> ...The spirit of the forest does not kill—not if no one else approaches. She eats sweet fruit and lies down wherever she pleases.
>
> Mother of wild beasts, untilled by a plough but full of food, sweet-smelling of perfume and balm—to her, the spirit of the forest, I offer praise.[3]

In Brahmanic culture, we find further associations of tree (or plant) with a particular deity. The sacred fig tree is associated with Lakshmi, goddess of fortune. This tree was worshipped by barren women in the hopes of conceiving a child. The same tree is also associated with Lakshmi's husband, Vishnu. The *vata (Ficus Indica)*, "banyan tree," because of its aerial roots and long life is a symbol of longevity, and in this capacity is associated with several different Hindu goddesses and gods, especially Brahma, Lakshmi, and Kuvera. As a tree that produces innumerable fruits and hence is evocative of fertility, it is associated with the goddess Sasthi. Many other examples could be cited. Durga or Vana Durga is a primitive forest goddess; she is also associated with plantain. Lakshmi is associated with the staple of rice.

In ancient folk religion a human woman is frequently linked with a tree, and the association often results in the tree's blossoming and bearing fruit. The pathiri ("yellow-flowered fragrant trumpet-flower") tree is reviled and ridiculed by women to yield flowers. A woman's look makes the sala tree bloom; her kick, the asoka tree; her embrace, the kura ("bottle-flower") tree; and her laughter makes jasmine creepers bloom. If a woman has her meal under a makilam tree, it will blossom.

In Buddhism this fertility motif reappears most obviously in the iconography at Sanchi and Bharat where large-breasted, sensuous women in association with a tree, are carved on the gates that lead into the temple precinct.

With so many of these associations of deity/tree and human being/tree suggesting fertility, the occurrence in the *Therigatha* poems of an association of Buddhist nuns and trees is striking in its incongruity. The celibate nun and the fertility goddess seem to occupy opposite ends of the spectrum. How did these nuns get into the picture?

The intermediary that links the fertility goddess and the nun is the Buddha. As is well-known, the Buddha became enlightened under the Bodhi tree. It is this "Tree of Wisdom" that becomes identified with the Buddha in story, teaching, and emerging iconography. Not only did the Buddha become enlightened while sitting under a tree, but according to less well-known legends, the Buddha was born and also died under special trees. The birth story, told in Chapter One, is that Maya, while on her way to her family home in Devadaha, stopped to pluck a branch from an asoka (*Saroca Indica*) tree. At that moment, she felt her first labor pains, lay down, and gave birth under that flowering tree. The story of the Buddha's death is that, while on pilgrimage in his eightieth year, and knowing that the end of his life was near, Gautama instructed Ananda to prepare a bed for him in the Sala Grove at Kushinara. As the Buddha lay down at the foot of twin sala trees, the trees burst into bloom out of season and rained flowers upon his body. It was beneath these twin trees that he died.

From these associations of trees with the Buddha, it is only one small step to an association of certain nuns of the *Therigatha* with particular trees. That the motif can appear in this new form shows both the energy of the primitive archetype, as well as the capacity of the newly emerging religion to incorporate and adapt elements from its earlier heritage and from popular mythology.

SOMA

Soma was the daughter of the minister of King Bimbisara. She would have been a woman of some status, as her father held a powerful position—something like a prime minister, but with religious responsibilities as well.

Soma first heard the Buddha preach on a visit he made to Rajagaha early in his teaching career. Her path followed a typical pattern of progressive involvement. After hearing the Buddha's discourse, she became a lay disciple and subsequently ordained as a nun. The final development along this trajectory was of her becoming an *arahant*, a "holy one."

Soma uttered her poem when, one day, she went out to sit beneath a tree to meditate. In India, "the earliest form of temple or place of worship was a tree. Originally there was no temple built to gods. Huge shady trees were supposed to be the abode of some unseen powers or gods."[4] As Soma was sitting under this tree, Mara appeared, and spoke the poem's first stanza. Soma contradicted him, with a response of great force. For her, it was self-evident that sexism arises from ignorance, and when "the great dark is torn apart," distinctions made on the basis of gender are seen as they really are, what in Pali is called *sammulisacca*, "conventional truth."

[Mara:]

> That place
> the sages gain
> is hard to reach.
> A mere woman can't get there.

[Soma:]

> What harm is it
> to be a woman
> when the mind is concentrated
> and the insight is clear?
>
> (If I asked myself:
> "Am I a woman
> or a man in this?"

then I would be speaking
Mara's language.)[5]

Everywhere the love of pleasure is destroyed,
the great dark is torn apart,
and Death,
you too
are destroyed.

SELA

She was born in Alavi, twelve miles from the great commercial center of Kasi, and named Sela, meaning rock or crag. Sela was the daughter of King Alavaka and was also known as Alavika, meaning "(a female) forest-dweller." As a young unmarried woman, she went one day with her father to hear the Buddha preach, and like her father, decided to become a disciple. Later she ordained as a nun and moved several hundred miles away from her home to Savatthi. Like Soma, Sela was sitting under a tree when Mara spoke her poem's first stanza to her.

There is a good tree story connected with Sela. Apparently, in a previous life, Sela had had a very good marriage, but eventually her husband died. Being old herself, she decided to travel among different religious groups and teach what life had taught her. Coming one day to the sacred Bodhi tree of a former Buddha, she thought to herself, "If the Buddha is unsurpassed, then may this tree show me his enlightenment!" Immediately, the tree blazed like gold, and all the sky shone. In awe, Sela fell to her knees and worshipped the tree. Then she sat down under its branches for seven days, on the seventh performing a ceremony of veneration to the Buddha.

This story is a striking variation on those in which the woman's kick, embrace, or laughter cause the tree to blossom. Here the tree gives forth not blossom or fruit, but light or flames. By this particular myth we may understand that Buddhism placed value not on the material prosperity of fertility, but on transcendent wisdom.

[Mara:]

There's no escape
in this world.

Why not enjoy yourself,
or you'll regret it
in the end.

[Sela:]

There may be no escape
in this world,
yet I have made it mine
by insight.
Evil One,
not knowing the way,
you make friends with
the dregs of society.[6]

Pleasures of the senses are
swords and stakes.
The elements of body and mind
are a chopping block for them.
So what you call delight
holds no thrill for me.

Everywhere the love of pleasure is destroyed,
the great dark is torn apart,
and Death,
you too are destroyed.

SUKKA

Sukka was from a wealthy family in Rajagaha. Her name means "bright" or "lustrous," and the poem makes a play on this meaning. When Sukka was a young girl, she heard the Buddha preach and joined the sangha as a lay disciple. Later she was ordained by Dhammadinna, the nun famous for her eloquence (see Chapter Four). Sukka practiced with great sincerity and attained *nirvana* in a short time. As she matured, her skill as a speaker grew until she was considered the equal of her teacher, Dhammadinna. Eventually she assumed the leadership of a large following of nuns.

One day, when she returned home with her companions from alms-round in Rajagaha, Sukka began to preach. She spoke so beautifully that her listeners were enchanted, and even a tree at the edge of the gathering was inspired to go striding through the streets and alleys of the town, praising her excellence and exclaiming this poem.

The Pali word for tree-spirit in Dhammapala's Commentary on Sukka's poem is *devata*, literally, "deity." It is feminine, as are all abstract nouns ending in "ta." But whether a tree-spirit is more usually conceived of as female, male, or neuter is a matter of dispute.[7] The other common word for tree-spirit is *yakkha*, of which *yakkhini* is the feminine form.

Whatever their gender, various tree spirits seem to have admired Sukka. In the *Samyutta Nikaya* another tree-spirit pays homage to her in this way: "A wise lay follower / gained a lot of merit. / He gave a robe to Sukka / who is free from all bonds."[8]

> What has happened
> to these people in Rajagaha?
> They are like drunks,
> they don't listen
> to Sukka preaching
> the Buddha's teaching.
>
> But the wise drink her words
> as travellers drink rain
> and never tire of their sweetness.
>
> Sukka you are light
> because of your bright mind.
>
> Concentrated,
> free of desire,
> you have conquered
> Mara and his forces.
>
> Bear this body,
> it is your last.

BUDDHIST NUNS AND THE MOON

If, in ancient Indian mythology, the tree was assigned a special place in the plant kingdom, the moon held a similar position of authority among the heavenly bodies. The moon waxes, wanes, disappears, and reappears. It is a symbol of becoming, of birth and death. The moon's cycle makes it the heavenly body connected with the rhythms of life. As such, it governs or mirrors all those spheres of nature that fall under the law of recurring cycles: the tides, plant life, the fertility of women, rain, human destiny. The moon's rhythms symbolically connect, unify, and explain these varied realities.

However, the moon's authority is not unrivaled, but is challenged by that of the sun. The sun is always the same, forever bright. It is the quintessential symbol of sheer light, of eternal laws that never change, of immortality. In the heat of the tropics it is often conceived of as a terrible force: blazing, war-like, destructive.

This tension between the moon and the sun has a parallel in the tension between the mythologies of the Indus and Aryan civilizations. In Indus Valley mythology, the lunar bull with his crescent horns was the foremost symbolic beast. But according to the system of the Vedas, "the place of honor went to the lion, who eats up the bull as the warrior drinks the *soma* and the sun consumes the light of the moon."[9] But the moon, by its very nature, does not die, and its mythic centrality could not be obliterated by the invading Aryans. Instead, Indus mythologies were taken over and assimilated into existing Aryan mythologies of both the sun and the moon.

The oldest Indo-Aryan root word connected with the heavenly bodies, *me*, gives pride of place not to the sun but to the moon. All the words relating to the moon in Indo-Aryan languages come from that root. For the Aryans, the moon's significance lay partially in the fact that it was the measure of time. The Sanskrit derivative of the root, *me*, is *mani*, "I measure."

Thus the Aryans, in common with ancient peoples worldwide, ordered their days, months, and years according to a lunar calendar. Rituals and sacrifices took place on the new and full moon days. That sacrifice and the moon were linked was no coincidence. In the Vedic system, the god Soma, identified with the moon, was linked with sacrifice. Soma was the counterpart of Tammuz—the Near Eastern god of dying—and carried the same associations. He was identified with the waxing and waning moon, with the bull tethered to the sacrificial post, and most of all with the sap, milk, and blood that flows through all life, which in the form of the intoxicating drink from the juice of the soma plant, is the ambrosia of immortal life. This juice is the counterpart on Earth of the drink of the gods, *amrita* ("*a*" meaning "non," and "*mrita*" meaning "death"—etymologically related to the Greek *ambrosia*).

The symbolism is complex and fascinating. The moon is both the god Soma and the vessel or cup which holds the immortal fluid. The lunar god controls the waters which circulate through the universe and become rain and dew. These waters in turn become vegetable sap, which becomes the milk of the cow, which in its final transmutation becomes blood.

In the Upanishadic tradition, the moon holds not the ambrosia of the gods but the souls who await rebirth. But the initiated are said to take the path not of the moon but of the sun. Therefore they are set free from illusions and ignorance. In this respect, the Buddhist system imitates the Upanishadic one in its transcendence of perpetual rebirth through cutting off darkness and ignorance.

In his excellent study of Oriental mythology, Joseph Campbell juxtaposes the age of lunar mythologies, calling these the age of the bull, with solar mythologies, the age of the lion. While Soma imitates Tammuz and to that extent partakes of the mythologies of an earlier age, the Vedic Aryans worshipped solar deities and the principles they represented. Those brahmans initiated into the Upanishadic disciplines and those "true brahmans" of Buddhism were, in their respective systems, wholly in line with Vedic-Aryan thought. Campbell writes:

> The mythology of the Buddha is of the Sun. He is termed the Lion of the Sakya Clan, who sits upon the Lion Throne. The symbol of his teaching is the Sun Wheel, and the reference of his doctrine is to a state that is no state, of which the only appropriate image is light.[10]

But this is only part of the picture. Both lunar and solar mythologies have been firmly documented for the period ca. 700 - 600 B.C.E., the early Upanishadic period which directly precedes and influences the Buddhist period. If the Vedic-Aryans had been in tension with the people of the Indus culture and if one of the indicators of that tension is opposing mythologies, then we find evidence of the co-existence of lunar and solar mythologies by the Upanishadic and Buddhist period.

Such evidence is found in the poems of the *Theragatha* and *Therigatha*. In these poems the enlightened mind is equated, not with the sun, but with the full moon unobscured by cloud. This is the dominant metaphoric use of the symbol of the moon. And, just as the enlightened mind is neither male nor female, so too, the moon is without gender and handled similarly in both collections of poems.

Several examples from the *Theragatha* illustrate how the full moon is used as a metaphor for enlightenment:

> Be like the moon a fortnight old in cloudless
> sky.[11]

> He goeth o'er the world a radiance shedding
> as when the moon comes free in cloudy
> sky.[12]

> The round of life renewed has ceased
> and naught of clinging doth remain
> E'en as the moon on the fifteenth day
> sails in clear sky without a stain.[13]

In only one poem, are lunar and solar imagery juxtaposed:

> As when th' obscuring clouds have drifted
> from the sky,
> The moon shines splendid even as the sun.[14]

Therefore we can say that Buddhist mythology does not ignore, deny, or supplant lunar mythology, but uses it selectively. Metaphorically, it is the moon on the fifteenth day, the full moon, that is honored. In this respect Buddhism tentatively integrates lunar mythology, but only to a point. Buddhism does not make use of the ancient Near Eastern symbolism of the dying god, of the moon as a symbol of becoming, of death and resurrection. As a symbol of becoming, the moon is supplanted by Mara or the intellectual concept of *samsara*, of birth and death. If this kind of lunar symbolism were used, it would not have positive connotations. The waxing and waning moon would be conceived as the enemy, just as Mara or *samsara* were the enemy.

These mythologies of the moon seem immensely complex in relation to the simple use of the metaphor of the full moon in the next two poems. But they have been presented in some detail to help us see that the metaphors we find in these poems cannot be fully appreciated apart from that culture.

MUTTA

Mutta means "free woman," free in the sense of enlightened. In the *Therigatha*, there are poems of two women named Mutta.

The Mutta who composed this poem came from a brahman family. She joined the sangha under Pajapati and learned how to meditate from her. One day, after Mutta had returned from her almsround, she did some chores and then went off to practice meditation. This poem came to her in a vision. She spoke it at the time, and later, when she had the deep experience that established her as an *arahant*, she spoke it again. Legend has it that when she was about to die she repeated the poem a third time.

> Mutta, free woman,
> be free
> as the moon is freed
> from the eclipse
> of the dragon Rahu's dark jaws.[15]

> With a free mind,
> in no debt,
> enjoy what has been given to you,
> this almsfood.

PUNNA

There is no particular story about Punna except that, like Mutta, she was from Savatthi and she too joined the nuns' sangha under Mahapajapati when she was twenty. Given these similarities, it is interesting that her poem should also be about the moon.

More directly than any other in the *Therigatha*, Punna's poem identifies the enlightened mind with the full moon. Such is the brilliance of the moon's light on the fifteenth day that it overpowers the darkness. This is the same power that allows the moon to free itself from the eclipse caused by the dragon Rahu. This symbolism of the moon indicates strength, but not invulnerability. There is darkness; there is ignorance; there is craving. But the full moon on the fifteenth day is the metaphor of triumph.

> Punna, be filled with all good things[16]
> like the moon on the fifteenth day.
> Completely, perfectly full
> of wisdom
> tear open
> the massive dark.

---

[1] E.W. Burlingame, tr. *Buddhaghosa's Dhammapada Commentary (Dhammapadatthakatha)*. 3 Vols. Harvard Oriental Series Vol. 28. (Cambridge: Harvard University Press, 1921), pp. 98-99.

[2] Sankar Sen Gupta, ed. *Tree Symbol Worship in India*. (Calcutta: Indian Publications, 1965), p. 58.

[3] Wendy O'Flaherty. *The Rig Veda: An Anthology*. (Harmondsworth, England: Penguin Books, Ltd., 1981), p. 242.

[4] Sankar Sen Gupta, ed. *Op Cit.*, p. 108.

[5] I have incorporated this stanza from the *Bhikkhunisamyutta* into the *Therigatha* poem, in order to bring additional original material by a given nun into this scant collection. Both poems share identical first stanzas. This stanza completes the *Bhikkhunisamyutta* poem. See: Leon M. Feer, ed. *Samyutta Nikaya of the Sutta Pitaka. Bhikkhuni Samyutta*. Vol. I. Book V. (London: Pali Text Society, 1973).

[6] This stanza is also from the *Bhikkhunisamyutta*. Sela's/Alivaka's poems in the *Therigatha* and *Bhikkhunisamyutta* versions have identical first and third stanzas. This stanza is the middle one in the *Bhikkhunisamyutta* version.

[7] Sankar Sen Gupta, ed. *Women in Indian Folklore*. (Calcutta: Indian Publications, 1969), p. 127.

[8] Leon M. Feer, ed. *Op. Cit.*, part 1-part 2, pp. 206, 216.

[9] Joseph Campbell. *The Masks of God: Oriental Mythology*. (New York: Penguin, 1970), p. 206.

[10] *Ibid.*, p. 255.

[11] Caroline Rhys Davids, tr. *Psalms of the Brethren*. (London: Pub. for the Pali Text Society by Henry Frowde, Oxford University Press Warehouse, 1913), p. 376.

[12] *Ibid.*, p. 322.

[13] *Ibid.*, p. 186.

[14] *Ibid.*, p. 406.

[15] Rahu, in Indian mythology, is described as a dark planet, a dragon, or a demon. He is called "the seizer" because he seizes the sun and moon, causing eclipses. An old story about him, taken from the *Mahabharata* is this: The gods were once drinking ambrosia, obtained from Vishnu. Having secretly taken the form of a god, the demon Rahu sought to drink also. But the sun and the moon reported the camouflage, and Vishnu cut off the demon's head. That head, great like the peak of a mountain, fell to the Earth, then rose again to the sky, roaring terribly. Since that time there has been a deadly enmity between Rahu and the sun and moon, and the immortal head still swallows them up, even today!

[16] Punna's name means "full," and her poem makes a play on this meaning to identify Punna's light and wisdom with that of the full moon.

CHAPTER ELEVEN

Dialogue Poems

The chief characteristic that unites the poems of the *Therigatha* is that they are all enlightenment poems, verses which proclaim a nun's attainment of the highest religious experience. This presupposes a further common characteristic—that these poems describe one individual's experience, and each is the utterance of one person. Sometimes, however, the poem is not presented as a continuous and connected whole. Some poems may have been spoken on different occasions and later incoherently pieced together. Examples include the poems of Uppalavanna and Kisagotami. Although not labeled in the original, these poems make a lot more sense if they are divided into units and labeled as to speaker.

More frequent than poems spoken by one person on different occasions are dialogues involving two or more speakers. Identifying the speakers in such poems makes the poems more vivid and easier to understand. We have already encountered a number of examples in previous chapters. Although attention has not been directed to them until now, these "dialogue poems" are rudimentary dramas, the roots of which go back another thousand years.

The dialogue or conversation hymns of the *Rig Veda* appear to be the origin of the Buddhist dialogue poem. The Sanskrit term for this genre is *akhyana*. These are fragments of narratives in the form of dialogues (*samvadas*) scattered throughout the *Rig Veda* (cf. 4.26-27, 10.108, 10.124, 10.135, 10.28, 10.51 etc.). Winternitz, citing H. Oldenberg, refers to them as *"akhyana hymns"* and suggests that there are about twenty of them.[1] Often these hymns relate to fertility and may have been part of a special ritual performance involving actors and dancers. They explore the relationship between men and women, mortal and immortal.[2] In subsequent ancient Indian poetry, poems with a structure like the dialogue hymns of the *Rig Veda* occur frequently. There are similar semi-epic and semi-dramatic poems, consisting chiefly or entirely of dialogues or conversations in the *Mahabharata*, in the *Puranas*, and especially in Buddhist literature.

The most famous of the *Rig Veda* dialogue hymns is a conversation between an immortal, the *aspara* water nymph Urvasti, and

Pururavas—her heroic, but mortal, husband. While the *Rig Veda* hymns are entirely in verse, to understand the conversation often presupposes knowledge of a complex myth. The outline of the Urvasti/Pururavas myth is that the nymph Urvasti loved Pururavas but promised that she would marry him only if he would agree to three conditions, one of which was that he would never let her see him naked. If she saw him naked, she would disappear. This agreed, they lived together for four years and had a son. But the Gandharvas, demigods of the same kingdom to which the water-nymphs belonged, wanted Urvasti back.

One night, as the couple was asleep, the Gandharvas stole two lambs which were tied to their bed. Awakened by the sound, Urvasti saw that the lambs were gone, and she cried out, "I have been robbed as if there were no man here!" Pururavas sprang out of bed, and in that moment, the Gandharvas produced a flash of lightning. Urvasti saw her mortal husband naked and vanished. Wandering in sorrow, Pururavas ultimately came to the lake where the water-nymphs lived, and Urvasti appeared to him. The hymn begins here. The following excerpt shows the dramatic quality and the compelling beauty which allowed the *akhyana* genre to evolve into variations like those in the Pali Buddhist literature.

[Pururavas:]
> My wife, turn your heart and mind to me. Stay here,
> dangerous woman, and let us exchange words. If we do
> not speak out these thoughts of ours they will bring us
> no joy, even on the most distant day.

[Urvasti:]
> What use to me are these words of yours? I have left
> you, like the first of the dawns. Go home again,
> Pururavas. I am hard to catch and hold, like the wind...

[Pururavas:]
> ...or like an arrow shot from the quiver for a prize, or
> like a racehorse that wins cattle, that wins hundreds.
> Even if there was no man with power there, they [the

Gandharvas] made the lightning flash and in their
frenzy thought to bleat like sheep.

She brought to her husband's father nourishing
riches, and whenever her lover desired her she came to
his home across from her dwelling place and took her
pleasure in him, pierced by his rod day and night.

[Urvasti:]

Indeed, you pierced me with your rod three times a day,
and filled me even when I had no desire. I followed
your will, Pururavas; you were my man, king of my
body.[3]

While the male and female roles are reversed and while renunciation is not a solution in a Vedic dialogue hymn, this selection ad-
dresses the theme of marital tension and separation, much like the
poem of Capa and her husband Kala (see Chapter Six). The tone of
the two poems is similar and there are even echoes of the same language (e.g. "dangerous woman"). While both are in verse, the language of the *Rig Vedic* is more earthy, the Pali poem more puritanical.

The Pali equivalent of the Sanskrit *akhyana* is *akkhana* meaning
"tale," or "narrative." H. Oldenberg defines *akhyana* as the verse portion of a type of narrative wherein, inside a general framework of
prose there appears, in emphasized passages, especially in the more
important speeches and replies, verses.[4] Winternitz sees no reason to
have *akhyana* refer only to narrative poetry that is a mixture of prose
and verse, but prefers to see *akhyana* as "ancient ballads" or "the ballad in general,"[5] by ballad meaning a narrative or song that tells a
story and which is typically presented as a conversation. Usually the
dialogue itself is sufficient to evoke the underlying story. When this
is not the case, a brief prose formula, a short introduction, and/or a
few prose sentences were often inserted.

In the oldest texts of the *Tipitaka* are poems modeled after the
akhyana. Yet the *Tipitaka*, while in various places mentioning a division of types according to nine "limbs": sermons in prose, sermons
in verse and prose, commentaries, verses, sayings, short speeches,
stories, miracle reports, and teachings in the form of question and

answer, does not include *akhyana* among these subdivisions. Technically, *akhyana* would fall under the division of sermons in verse and prose. But this doesn't sufficiently capture the genre. Winternitz elaborates on the full range of this literary form:

> Side by side with prose sermons into which occasional verses are inserted, or sermons in verse but with a prose framework, we also find forms, popular from time immemorial, both of pure dialogue and of the *akhyana* or the ballad, in which the dialogue-stanzas alternate with narrative-stanzas, and lastly of the *akhyana* composed of a mixture of prose and verse—all forms with which we are familiar from the ancient Brahmanical and epic poetry.[6]

In the *Therigatha*, the dialogue is typically a simple, one-time exchange between two speakers. These can be exchanges between a teacher and a disciple, a husband and a wife, Mara and a nun, or among several speakers. The reader will recall the exchanges between the Buddha and Sundari-Nanda (Chapter One), Patacara and her thirty nuns (Chapter Two), Mara and Khema, and Mara and Uppalavanna (Chapter Three), the Buddha and Ubbiri, Patacara and Pancasata Patacara, Kisagotami and the Buddha, Mara and Kisagotami (Chapter Five), Capa and Kala (Chapter Six), Abhaya and Padumavati (Chapter Eight), the Buddha and Abhaya, and the three sisters Cala, Upacala, and Sisupacala and Mara (Chapter Nine), Mara and Sela (Chapter Ten). To this list we add the poems of this last chapter.

The *Therigatha* dialogue poems do not identify the speakers at the outset of their lines, as we expect in the manuscript of a play. Rather, the speakers are revealed in the content or are implied by the context. The only exception to this is in prose portions of the text, where occasionally the Buddha or Mara is named as speaker. Quotation marks aren't used in Pali. In the translations in this volume, the speaker has been named in brackets.

In this chapter I have included representative examples of Pali Buddhist dialogue poems from the *Therigatha*. The first is a conversation between Mara and Vijira. Dialogues where Mara is one of the two speakers are a common sub-genre within the dialogue poem type. The second poem is a dialogue between the slave girl, Punnika, and the brahman, Udakasuddhika. The third poem, a dialogue between the enlightened nun, Subha, and a lecherous man, is the longest included in this collection. The fourth and final poem of this chapter is the most elaborate example of a dialogue poem; it includes a narrator and no fewer than seven other speakers.

VAJIRA

[Mara:]

Who put this living being together?
Where is the maker?
Where does this being come from?
Where will it end?

[Vajira:]

What's this "being" you go on about?
That's your delusion.
We are nothing but the *skandhas*.
There's no "being" to be found here.

It's like this:
A certain combination of parts
is called by the name "chariot,"
so with the *skandhas*—
the elements of mind and body,
it's common usage to say "a being."

It is suffering that exists,
suffering that endures,
suffering that disappears.

Nothing but suffering exists.
Nothing but suffering comes to an end.

Then Mara, Death himself, thought, "Vajira knows me," and, sad and dejected, vanished.[7]

PUNNIKA

Punnika was the daughter of a slave, and a slave herself. She was the one hundredth child born into the household of Anathapindika, the wealthy lay follower of the Buddha who had purchased Jeta Grove to be used as one of the earliest Buddhist monasteries.

Originally, the word *dasa* (lit. "non-Aryan") was applied to hostile non-Aryan people who have been equated with the Dravidians and Mundra-speaking pre-Aryans.[8] After the Aryan conquest, *dasa* came to mean "slave," "servant," or any member of the *sudra*, the lowest caste. As the Aryan conquest spread into eastern India, more and more of these aboriginal people, who had previously lived as peaceful townspeople and peasant farmers, became available as laborers. These people were owned in much the same way as cattle were owned.

The "proto-Dravidians"[9] of western India, having lived as townspeople and peasants, not as warriors, were easier to reduce to slavery than the peoples of the Ganges valley forests. The Nagas were forest-dwellers who gained their livelihood as food-gatherers. They were difficult to conquer or reduce to slavery on account of their protective, dense forest habitat. While caste distinctions, including the distinction of *sudra*, had come to the Indus valley population many centuries earlier, caste did not begin to make its appearance in the Ganges valley until the fifth century B.C.E.

Some of the eastward conquering Aryan tribes did continue to function without a caste system, while others used only the *arya-sudra*, free vs. slave distinction. *Dasa* or *sudra* were not bought and sold, though this was not on account of an ethical stand against the evils of slavery, but because private ownership had not evolved to this degree of complexity. Chattel slavery as known in Europe and the United States never developed in India.

By the Buddha's lifetime in the Ganges region, wealthy householders like Anathapindika had numerous slaves, and in the Pali literature slave-ownership is a subject for tales of both kindness and brutality. Female domestic slaves like Punnika were required to perform menial but necessary household duties such as husking paddy, pounding rice, drawing water, and going to market. Some slave women belonged to the harems of wealthy men. Others were entertainers, skilled in song and dance.

Punnika's job was to carry water, and she achieved the so-called first stage of the Buddhist path while still a slave. This occurred after she heard a discourse by the Buddha, the "Lion's Roar." It was on the basis of this insight that Punnika had the confidence to challenge the brahman Udakasuddhika. He believed in the efficacy of purification by water, a common belief among Aryan brahmans.

Later, Punnika approached the Buddha saying that she wanted to become his disciple. Though he was about to leave for Savatthi, she asked that he postpone his departure and help her achieve her end. As a slave, Punnika could not be admitted into the nuns' sangha. She would first have to be granted freedom. When the idea was broached to him, Anathapindika agreed not only to free Punnika, but to adopt her as his own daughter. From these three examples, first in relation to the brahman Udakasuddhika, next with the Buddha, and finally with Anathapindika, we sense that Punnika was a woman able to convince those in authority to support her cause. The clarity of her faith allowed her to obtain her freedom, to receive full ordination, and ultimately to become an *arahant*.

[Punnika:]

> I am a water carrier.
> Even in the cold
> I have always gone down to the water,
> frightened of punishment
> or the angry words
> of high-class women.
> So what are you afraid of, brahman,
> that makes you go down to the water?
> Your limbs shake with the bitter cold.

[Udakasuddhika:]

> But you know why, Punnika.
> I am doing good to prevent evil.
> Anyone young or old who has done
> something bad
> is freed by washing in water.

[Punnika:]

Whoever told you
you are freed from evil by washing?
The blind leading the blind!
In that case all frogs and turtles
would go to heaven,
and water snakes and crocodiles
and the rest of the water creatures.
Butchers of sheep, butchers of pigs,
fishers and trappers,
thieves, executioners,
and other wrongdoers
would be freed from their bad karma
by washing in water.
If these streams carried away all your old evil
they would carry away your virtue too.
You would be separated from both.
Don't do that thing
the fear of which
leads you down to the water.
Stop now, brahman,
save your skin from the cold.

[Udakasuddhika:]

Lady,
I was on the wrong road
and you brought me back
to the great road.
I will give you the robe
I bathed in.

[Punnika:]

Keep the robe;
I don't want it.
If you are afraid of pain,
if you don't like it,
do nothing evil,
either openly or in secret.

For if you do,
even if you get up and run away
you won't escape its pain.
If you are afraid of pain,
if you don't like it,
take refuge in the Buddha,
the Dharma and the Sangha.
Train in the precepts.
This is good.

[Udakasuddhika:]
I take refuge in the Buddha,
the Dharma and the Sangha.
I train in the precepts.
This is good.

Once I was only Brahma's kin.
I had the three knowledges[10]
and great learning.
Now I am a true brahman.
I am washed clean.

SUBHA

Subha means "bright," "shining," or "beautiful." She was a strikingly lovely woman from an eminent brahman family of Rajagaha. Instead of marrying, she became a nun under Pajapati and she liked to go walking alone in the woods.

In keeping with the larger tradition of wandering renunciants, the Buddha's teaching emphasized the desirability of living apart, of "wandering alone like a rhinoceros." The third of the four *nissayas*, the most important guidelines for Buddhist monastic living, was to dwell at the foot of a tree.[11] Such an environment was considered the ideal place for meditation. In the case of nuns, however, the third *nissaya* was dropped, after a nun was raped in the woods. The *Cullavagga* states, "Now at that time, nuns dwelt in the forest and men of abandoned life violated them. They told this matter to the Blessed One. [He replied:] 'A nun is not to adopt the forest life.'"[12]

Henceforth, Buddhist nuns were no longer permitted to dwell at the foot of a tree, nor were they allowed to enter a village alone, cross on a ferry alone, go out at night alone, travel alone, or bathe where men or prostitutes bathed.

The circumstances of Subha's poem suggest that her experience predated these restrictions. Subha went to the woods to walk and meditate, and, on the occasion of this poem, was confronted by a stranger who wanted her sexually. Though this is a potentially terrifying situation, their interaction has a farcical side, exaggerated by the length and elaborateness of their dialogue. This potential rapist, whom we sense to be rather young, displays, under pressure of the situation, a wild imagination and capacity for fast talking. And Subha, in turn, uses the occasion, if not to actively proselytize, then at least to display her insight.

The resolution of their confrontation is completely unexpected. If, to us, their encounter seems comical due to the elaborateness of their speeches, Subha perceived the situation otherwise. She must have felt in danger or she wouldn't have taken the course of action she did—plucking out her own eye. Her act can be interpreted in several ways.

Clearly, Subha has no sexual interest in this man. She demonstrates her ability to transcend the vulnerability of the flesh and physically mutilates herself. Having gained the "inner eye," Subha has no attachment to her outer eye. On another level, Subha's action may be seen as a radical gesture of compassion intended to bring the potential rapist to self-awareness. Such interpretations are within the realm of realism, but the poem evokes psychological or mythical interpretation as well.

Subha's act of partially blinding herself calls to mind the *Oedipus* myth. Oedipus, having lived out his destiny—killing his father and marrying his mother—stabs out both of his eyes. Is there any mythical parallel to Subha's experience? To the extent that both link human sexuality and sight, perhaps we may answer yes. From such a point of view, Subha's half-seeing may be interpreted as a blindness to the idea that passion is an integral dimension of human experience. But the faithful *Theravadin* Buddhist would interpret this differently. She or he would link, not sexuality and sight, but renunciation and sight/insight, and would note the Buddha's act of

restoring Subha's sight as a significant miracle—one of the rare heal-
ing miracles attributed to him. Furthermore, such a person would
repudiate the view that passion is a fact of an *arahant's* experience.
Having already attained arahantship by the time of her encounter,
Subha had eliminated all obsessions of the mind, chief among which
was passion.

> The nun Subha was walking in the lovely Jivakamba
> woods when a lecherous man stopped her. She said:

[Subha:]

> What have I done to you?
> Why do you stand in my way?
> It's not right to touch a woman who has left home.
> The Wellfarer taught this strict discipline,
> and my own teacher too.
> I live in purity,
> so why do you block me?
> Your mind is out of control,
> full of passion.
> But I am serene;
> my passion is gone.
> I am clear
> and my mind is free in every way.
> Why do you block me?

[Man:]

> You're young and innocent.
> What will leaving home do for you?
> Throw away your saffron robe.
> Come! Enjoy the flowering woods.
> Sweetness falls from the tall trees.
> Flower pollen whirls all around.
> The beginning of spring is a time of joy.
> Come! Enjoy the flowering woods.
> The treetops are in blossom
> and they call out when the wind shakes them.
> What pleasure will you have

if you go all alone to the woods?
You want to go without a companion
into the lonely, huge, frightening forest
where savage animals live?
Cow elephants roused by bull elephants
shatter the peace.

But you will be like a golden doll,
like a water nymph from Cittaratha.[13]
There will be no one to compare with you.
You will shine in muslin from Kasi.
If you lived in the woods with me
I would do what you wanted.
No one is dearer to me than you—
spirit creature with slow-moving eyes.
Let me make you happy.
Come! Live in a house,
in the calm of a palace.
Let women serve you.
You will wear fine muslin
put on flowers and make-up.
I will dress you with gold,
pearls, and precious stones.
Climb onto a fragrant bed of carved sandalwood
spread with clean and beautiful covers
and an expensive, fleecy, new quilt.
Just as the blue lotus
rising from the water
is visited only by spirits,
you, nun, will go to old age,
with your limbs untouched.

[Subha:]

This fragile body is full of death
and headed for the grave.
What do you see of value here
that makes you stare at me?
You're out of your mind.

[Man:]

Your eyes are like those of a doe
like those of a spirit inside a mountain.
They excite me.
They are like the bud of a blue lotus,
pure, shining.
I am aroused more than before.
Even if you were far away
I couldn't forget you,
your long eyelashes,
your pure gaze.
No eyes are dearer to me than yours
spirit creature with slow-moving eyes.[14]

[Subha:]

You're heading down the wrong path.
You want the moon as your toy
and to leap over Mount Meru.[15]
But you are chasing after the Buddha's child.
There is nothing in heaven or earth
that I want.
I don't even know about desire—
what is it?—
only that the root
has been cut out
through the Great Way.
It has been scattered like a heap of coals.
It's like a bowl of poison to me.
I don't even see it—
what is it?—
only that the root
has been cut out
through the Great Way.
Try to seduce someone
who hasn't seen this
and hasn't sat by a teacher.
But if you try this on me,
you will be frustrated.

My attention is unshaken
by joy or pain,
praise or blame.
I know there is no happiness
in anything born from a cause,
and I cling to nothing.
I follow the Wellfarer
and travel on the great Eightfold Way.
The arrow is out.
There are no obsessions in my mind.
Having gone into the empty house,
I rejoice.
I have seen brightly painted puppets
made to dance by sticks and strings.
When you take off these sticks and strings,
throw them away,
scatter the puppets,
and break them into pieces
so that you can't find them,
what is left for the mind to fix on?
So too with this puny body—
it doesn't exist apart from its qualities.
What is there for the mind to fix on?
You have been confused
looking at a painted picture on a wall
made with yellow pigment.
Human knowledge is useless.
Blind man, you are chasing an empty thing,
an illusion,
a tree of gold at the end of a dream,
a puppet-show in a crowd.
An eye is just a little ball in a socket
with a bubble in the middle,
tears, secretions.

Then this woman, who was so lovely to behold, plucked
out her eye. She was not attached to it. "Here, take this

eye," she said, and gave it to him. His passion died then
and there and he begged forgiveness.

[Man:]

> Make yourself whole again, religious woman.
> This won't happen again.
> Coming up against you
> is like embracing fire,
> or grabbing a poisonous snake.
> Make yourself whole again.
> Forgive me.

Then he let her go and she went to the excellent
Buddha. Seeing him, her eye was restored.

SUNDARI

I have saved the wonderful poem of Sundari for last. Although it is
attributed to Sundari, it could just as well be attributed to several
other of the seven speakers—to the enlightened nun Vasetthi, to
Sundari's mother (unnamed), to Sundari's teacher (unnamed), or to
Sundari's father, Sujata, as all speak a significant number of lines.
Containing so many characters, the poem is in fact a rudimentary
drama. And just as, when attending a dramatic presentation in a for-
eign language, such as an opera or a Japanese *Noh* play, one wants a
list of the characters and a synopsis of the plot in order to understand
what's going on, one needs the same thing in this poem-drama.
Here it is:

CHARACTERS (IN ORDER OF APPEARANCE):

Sujata (Sundari's father, a brahman)
Vasetthi (an enlightened nun)
Sundari's mother
A charioteer (under the service of Sujata)
Sundari (a young woman)
Sundari's teacher
An onlooker from Savatthi
The Buddha (Siddhartha Gautama)

PLOT

The story opens with Sundari's father, the brahman Sujata, over-come by grief over the death of his son. Wandering about, he meets the nun Vasetthi. Vasetthi, who has herself known the grief of los-ing seven children, teaches Sujata the way to end suffering through the Dharma of Siddhartha Gautama. Sujata seeks out Gautama and in only three nights attains *nirvana*. Sujata's charioteer, who has ac-companied him, is sent back home to inform Sujata's wife that he has renounced the world.

At the brahman's home, having learned the good news about her husband, Sujata's wife wants to reward the charioteer for his service, but he too has decided to leave the world and will accept no payment.

In the next scene, Sundari's mother tells Sundari of Sujata's deci-sion. With her brother dead, now she, Sundari, is the heir to the family fortune. But Sundari wants to follow her father's path by re-nouncing the world and embracing the Buddha's teaching. Her mother does not resist her daughter's aspiration.

The next scene takes place some time later. Sundari has been studying under a Buddhist nun in Benares, whom she reveres as a great woman and a spiritual friend. Now, at last, Sundari has attained her heart's desire, *nirvana*, and she wants to proclaim her achieve-ment before Gautama himself. Her teacher encourages her to go to the Buddha, who is in Savatthi.

The last scene opens with an onlooker from Savatthi announcing Sundari's arrival. The young woman Sundari proudly presents her achievement and the Buddha welcomes her and acknowledges her realization.

Sundari's poem is unique for several reasons. It is the only example in the *Therigatha* of a father's grief for the loss of his child, and is therefore a moving counterpoise to the many examples of a mother's grief. In the first dialogue, Sujata's conversation with Vasetthi is a rare example of a man, and a brahman at that, seeking the advice and guidance of a woman. Sundari's poem is also special and uplift-ing in the lovely dialogue with which it ends, where Sundari an-nounces that she is the Buddha's daughter, "your true child, born of your mouth." As such, she is completely related to and identified with the Enlightened One and is thus completely free.

[Sujata:]

Lady,
once
after you had left your dead children
at the charnel ground
exposed and to be eaten,
you grieved day and night
more than you could stand.
Vasetthi, now
that you have left seven children in all
why don't you grieve?

[Vasetthi:]

Brahman, in the past,
hundreds of children
and numberless kin
of yours and mine
have been left
exposed and to be eaten.
Now, though I am the same woman,
I know freedom from birth and death
and do not grieve or weep.

[Sujata:]

This is a startling thing to say, Vasetthi.
Whose teaching do you know?

[Vasetthi:]

Brahman, near the city of Mithila
the Enlightened One
has taught the Dharma to the living
so that suffering is left behind.
Brahman, I have heard that *arahant* teach—
there is no basis for rebirth—

and knowing the truth there,
I have driven away the grief for my children.

[Sujata:]

Then I will go to the city of Mithila
and perhaps the Blessed One
will free me from my suffering.

[Narrator:]

The brahman saw the Buddha,
who is completely free,
and has no basis for rebirth.
The Sage who has reached
the far shore of suffering
taught him the Way:
pain,
the cause of pain
the end of pain
and the great Eightfold Way
leading to the stilling of pain.

Because he found the truth there
it was a joy
to set out into homelessness.

After three nights
Sujata touched
the three knowledges.

[Sujata:]

Charioteer, take this chariot home.
Wish my wife good health,
and tell her the brahman
has set out into homelessness.

[Narrator:]

After three nights

Sujata touched
the three knowledges.

[Sundari's Mother:]
For the news that my husband
has the three knowledges
I give you this horse, this chariot,
and one thousand pieces of gold—
a full bowl.

[Charioteer:]
Lady,
keep the horse, the chariot
and the gold.
I too am leaving home
to join that man of marvelous wisdom.

[Sundari's Mother:]
Sundari,
your father has set out into homelessness
leaving behind the elephants,
cows, horses, jewels,
and all the wealth of his house.
Enjoy these riches.
You are the heir now.

[Sundari:]
My father set out into homelessness
out of grief for his son,
leaving behind these elephants,
cows, horses, jewels
and all the wealth of his house.
I too grieve for my brother.
I too am setting out into homelessness.

[Sundari's Mother:]
Sundari,
may you find what you long for.

Gleanings and leftover food,
a robe of rag
from the trash heap—
these are enough.
In the next world you will be free
of all the mind's obsessions.

[Sundari to her teacher:]
Great woman,
as I train,
the eye of heaven becomes clear.
I know where I have lived before
in previous lives.
Following you, my spiritual friend,
jewel of the order of nuns,
I have realized the three knowledges.
The Buddha's teaching has been done.

Great teacher,
let me go to Savatthi
I'll roar a lion's roar [16]
in the presence of the Buddha.

[Sundari's teacher:]
Sundari,
go and see the golden teacher
with his golden skin
who tames the wildness of our minds
and is enlightened,
unafraid.

[An Onlooker:]
Look! Sundari is coming.
Free, free of desire and its chains,
she will not be reborn.
Her mind is free of clinging.
Her task is done.

[Sundari to Buddha:]

> I am your disciple Sundari
> and I have come from Kasi to pay homage.
> Buddha, teacher,
> I am your daughter,
> your true child,
> born of your mouth.
> My mind is free of clinging.
> My task is done.

[Buddha:]

> Then welcome, welcome to you,
> great woman.
> The tamed come this way
> to pay homage to their teacher's feet.
> free of desire and its chains,
> your mind is free of clinging.
> Your task is done.

---

[1] M. Winternitz. *A History of Indian Literature*. Vol. I. (New Delhi: Oriental Book Reprint Corp., 1977), p. 100.

[2] Wendy O'Flaherty. *The Rig Veda*. (Middlesex, England: Penguin Books, Ltd., 1981), p. 245.

[3] Translation by Wendy O'Flaherty. *Ibid.*, p. 245.

[4] H. Oldenberg. "The Prose and Verse Type of Narrative and the Jatakas." *Journal of the Pali Text Society*. 1912, p. 19.

[5] M. Winternitz. *Op. Cit.*, Vol. II. p. 93.

[6] *Ibid.*, p. 93.

[7] This is a second example in this collection from the *Samyutta Nikaya. Bhikkhuni Samyutta* v. 10.

[8] I. Shekhar. *Sanskrit Drama: Its Origin and Decline*. (New Delhi: Munshiram Mancharlal Publishers Ltd., 1977), p. 21.

[9] Several similarities are so striking between the Indus Valley people and the Dravidians of southern India that some scholars refer to the Indus valley population as "Proto-Dravidians." (*Ibid.*, p. 21).

[10] *Tevijjo*, literally the three knowledges, was originally a Sanskrit term which described the brahman's special knowledge. The brahman Suddhika uses the term in that sense, perhaps unaware that the word was also adopted by the Buddhists to indicate their spiritual achievement.

[11] The four *nissayas* for Buddhist monks were (1) to live by begging, (2) to wear rags, (3) to live under a tree, (4) to use cow's urine as medicine. Buddhist nuns observed the first, second, and fourth *nissaya*.

[12] Max Müller, ed. *Vinaya Texts*. Part III. T.W. Rhys Davids and H. Oldenberg, tr. *Sacred Books of the East*. Vol. XX. (Oxford: Clarendon Press, 1885), *Kullavagga* X 23.

[13] In the Vedas, *asparas* (Sanskrit) are water nymphs found by rivers and holy pools. Later they metamorphose into heavenly beings. In the famous Buddhist Ajanta cave murals, *accharas* (Pali) are depicted as air spirits. They are the wives of the *asuras* and it is likely that their origin is the Indus civilization, where female priestesses and holy baths played a central role in religious ceremonies.

[14] *Kinnari*—lit. "spirit creature." This is another fairy, half-human, half-animal. Unlike the *accharas*, who are always female, *kinnaris* can be either male or female.

[15] Mount Meru is the dwelling place of gods and spirits in ancient Indian mythology. The topmost peak of Mount Meru—Mount Kailasa—is the retreat of Siva. Unlike Mount Olympus of ancient Greek mythology, Mount Meru is not an actual geographical site.

[16] A "lion's roar" is a proclamation of accomplishment, a song of victory.

The Legacy of the First Buddhist Women

Why are we interested 2,500 years later in the first Buddhist women? What are the legacies of their lives and poetry? There are several possible answers.

First, in this age where there is a headlong rush worldwide towards getting and spending, where the shopping mall has replaced the foot of the tree or the temple or church as the place of meditation and prayer, where a woman's appearance is her foremost concern, we are struck by the nuns of the *Therigatha* who took a different path. Those of us in the East or West who have had the good fortune to live in the "palace" of material well-being, also know that even in prosperity there is *dukkha*—pain. In common with Siddhartha Gautama and with the nuns of the *Therigatha*, we have asked ourselves: Is there a life beyond the illusions of materialism? Is there a way to overcome pain? The first legacy of the lives and poems of the *Therigatha* is the clear evidence that our bodies, our cars, our monthly credit and loan payments are not all that we are made of. There is another way, a way not simply followed but co-created by women at the birth of one of the world's great religious traditions.

Second, not only did these women turn away from materialistic lives; they turned towards a spiritual principle. Although their lives took many forms, the women of the *Therigatha* shared one significant trait. Through direct personal experience, each realized the truth in the phrase: "Look within, thou art the Buddha," and their poems are the record and expression of this. A second legacy of the original Buddhist nuns is an indisputable spiritual accomplishment.

Third is the legacy of their simple way of life. In common with the monks, these women lived on seven requisites and ate one meal a day. Relative to the more austere practices of that time, their's was not considered an ascetic, but a "middle path" between indulgence and asceticism. Nevertheless, this was and is a lifestyle vastly different from that which many Westerners take for granted. The model offered by the first Buddhists and followed by the faithful in *Theravadin* Buddhist countries to this day, is a model of "sustainability." In that era, simplicity was chosen because it was conducive to spiritual development. Though no less true today, the example of the simple way of life of the first Buddhist nuns has a special relevance in this time when we are destroying the Earth through our gross patterns of consumption. I am not suggesting that we try to live on seven requisites or eat just one meal a day, but that we can benefit immensely from their attitude of simplicity and apply the principles represented by that attitude to become more aware of what we truly need to sustain ourselves and our global village.

Most sources hold that the Buddha's dying words were to "be a light unto yourself," an idea complemented by the earliest Buddhist teaching on "no views" and discussed in Chapter Nine. This teaching suggests that we not seek to embrace a particular doctrine, faith, ideology, or form. In that spirit, it must be noted that the original nuns' sangha, although radical in its position on women relative to society, was sexist in many respects. Its rules were sexist and the obstacles to women's achievement were significant. As women and men continue to embrace Buddhism today, and especially as Westerners embrace a tradition so different from our own, we should take care not to tolerate sexism in the Buddhist institutions with which we are affiliated, nor perpetuate discrimination as new structures are invented. While we must applaud both the efforts to recreate a new order of nuns through full ordination, and the enthusiasm and energy that has been poured into Buddhist women's journals, books, and conferences over the last two decades, we must not lose sight of the facts. The old form didn't sustain women over the long haul; the *bhikkhuni* sangha of the *Theravadin* died out. Without significant changes, it will not sustain us now. Sexist rules, hierarchical structures, sexual exploitation of women by so-called celibate and/or enlightened teachers, monasticism that excludes women and children, and other oppressive institutional structures like these must give way to new forms supportive of women's full participation in and opportunity for complete realization. It is not that women cannot surmount these institutional obstacles. The nuns of the *Therigatha* and the successes of some women within the Buddhist sangha today attest to this. We must think for ourselves.

The fourth legacy is women's spiritual authority—the authority to lead, to teach, to publish, to hold any and all positions within institutions, and to control one's own body, mind, and spirit and all that we create. Spiritual authority is not simply an individual matter; it pertains to social structures. The social structures of sixth century B.C.E. India were somewhat supportive of women's spiritual development. However, in the succeeding centuries those same structures lapsed into rigid and hierarchical patterns that diminished and eventually obliterated women's self-expression.

What structure should we seek? Abhirupa-Nanda's poem provides a clue. The poem cautions us to:

> Get rid of the tendency
> to judge yourself
> above, below, or
> equal to others.

The poem suggests that what we must first set right is our attitude towards ourselves, not ranking ourselves in relation to others. If we apply this same ideal to social structures, we would not seek institutions where women, having been dominated by men, now become the dominators. Riane Eisler points to a possible way:

> When our ancestors began to ask the eternal questions (Where do we come from before we are born? Where do we go after we die?) they must have noted that life emerges from the body of a woman. It would have been natural for them to image the universe as an all-giving Mother from whose womb all life emerges and to which, like the cycles of vegetation, it returns after death to be again reborn. When the first evidence of such societies was unearthed in the nineteenth century, it was concluded that they must have been "matriarchal." Then, when the evidence did not seem to support this conclusion, it again became customary to argue that human society always was—and always will be—dominated by men. But if we free ourselves from the prevailing models of reality [in Buddhism one would say "free ourselves from dualistic thought"], it is evident that there is another logical alternative: that there can be societies in which difference is not necessarily equated with inferiority or superiority.[1]

Riane Eisler's model is consistent with Abhirupa-Nanda's poem. Eisler re-examines human society from a gender-holistic perspective, defining two basic models: the "dominator model"—which ranks one-half of humanity over the other, and the "partnership model"— in which "social relations are primarily based on the principle of linking rather than ranking."[2] Eisler posits a cultural evolution of Western societies from a partnership model to a domination model. Marija Gimbutas' research confirms that the Old European societies that worshipped the life-generating and nurturing powers of the universe were interrupted by Indo-Aryan people who, as herders and warriors, worshipped the "lethal power of the blade."[3] Decades of archeological and linguistic research suggest that these same Indo-Aryan peoples spread throughout the Indian subcontinent, beginning circa 1500 B.C.E., and that they may have been the destroyers of the native Indus civilization.[4] Although the greater availability of data on Western societies makes it possible to document this shift in more detail through the analysis of Western cultural evolution, Eisler goes on to say that "there are also indications that this change in direction from a partnership to a dominator model was roughly paralleled in other parts of the world."[5]

A fifth legacy of the lives and poems of the *Therigatha* is the record itself as an invaluable source of non-Western material on ancient women. This is some of the oldest historical material by and about women. For this reason alone, the *Therigatha* is a truly special body of work. In addition, it is material that provides support for the thesis that a cultural shift occurred not only in old Europe but in ancient India as well, a shift from women's empowerment and spiritual authority to their disenfranchisement.

To conclude, the legacy of the first Buddhist nuns is that everyone should be her or his own light. This means not to imitate but to use the example of these creative women to question all the veils cast by materialism, consumerism, and violent aggression. Each of us can realize the highest truths and we are called on to manifest these truths in our own lives. If we seek this in full sincerity, the nuns of the *Therigatha* are teaching us still.

---

[1] Riane Eisler. *The Chalice and the Blade*. (San Francisco: Harper and Row, 1987), pp. xvi-xvii.

[2] *Ibid.*, p. xvii.

[3] Marija Gimbutas. "The First Wave of Eurasian Steppe Pastoralists into Copper Age Europe." *The Journal of Indo-European Studies* 5. (Winter 1977), p. 281. See also: *The Language of the Goddess.* (San Francisco: Harper and Row, 1989).

[4] J.P. Mallory. *In Search of the Indo-Europeans: Language, Archeology, and Myth.* (London: Thames and Hudson Ltd., 1989), p. 45.

[5] Riane Eisler. *Op. Cit.*, p. xvii.

Rules of the Nuns' Sangha

The nuns' sangha modeled itself after the monks' sangha, only the nuns' rules and regulations were stricter. The purpose of these stricter rules was to keep women's supposedly more wayward nature under control and to keep final authority in the hands of the monks.

The Buddha was concerned about the consequences of allowing women the privilege of ordination and the opportunity to control the daily affairs of their own sangha. He feared that the formation of such a community could negatively affect the well-being of his total following, not to mention the receptivity of others to his new message. His supposed prediction at the time of his decision, addressed to Ananda, was:

> If...women had not received permission to renounce their homes and enter into homelessness under the dhamma and discipline proclaimed by the Tathagata, then would the pure religion...have lasted long, the good law would have stood for a thousand years. But since...women have now received that permission, the pure religion...will not last so long, the good law will now stand fast for only five hundred years. Just...as houses in which there are many women but few men are easily violated by robber burglars; just so...under whatever dhamma and discipline women are allowed to renounce their homes and enter into homelessness, that religion will not last long. And just...as when the disease called mildew falls upon a field of rice in fine condition, that rice does not continue long; just so...under whatever dhamma and discipline women are allowed to renounce their homes and enter into homelessness, that religion will not last long...And just...as a man in anticipation builds an embankment to a great reservoir, beyond which the water should not overpass, just even so...have I laid down these Eight Chief Rules for the bhikkhunis, not to be disregarded throughout their whole life.[1]

This is both a prediction and the explanation given as to why strict rules were needed by the nuns' sangha. The additional rules can be broken down into several distinct categories. First there were the Eight Special Rules, the acceptance of which was the prerequisite to Mahapajapati's ordination, and the establishment of the order of nuns. They were "special" in the sense that they were unique to the nuns only. The Eight Special Rules were:

1) A nun, even of a hundred years' standing, shall respectfully greet, rise up in the presence of, bow down before, and perform all proper duties towards a monk ordained even a day.

2) A nun is not to spend the rainy season in a district where there is no monk.

3) Every half-moon, a nun is to await two things from the order of monks—the date of the *Uposatha* ceremony and the time the monks will come to give teaching.

4) After the rains retreat, the nuns are to hold *Pavarana* [to inquire as to whether any faults have been committed] before both sanghas, that of the monks and that of the nuns, in respect to what has been seen, what has been heard, and what has been suspected.

5) A nun who has been guilty of a serious offense must undergo the *manatta* discipline before both sanghas, that of the monks and that of the nuns.

6) When a novice has trained for two years in the six precepts [the first five precepts plus the precept of taking one meal a day before noon], she should seek ordination [the *Upasampada* initiation] from both sanghas.

7) A nun is not to revile or abuse a monk under any circumstances.

8) Admonition by nuns of monks is forbidden; admonition of nuns by monks is not forbidden.[2]

In addition to the Eight Special Rules, there was the *bhikkhuni-vibhanga*, or collection of rules (lit. "nuns' division" or "nuns' classification") that was patterned after the *bhikkhuvibhanga*, the monks' collection of rules. It is a separate book of rules to be observed solely by the nuns. Because the extant *bhikkhunivibangha* contains only 84 rules, we may regard this present form as an abridged version of a formerly more complete collection for nuns. In addition to the 84 rules, the nuns were responsible for observing 227 rules equivalent to those found in the monks' collection of rules. The monks observed a total of 227 rules, the nuns a total of 311.

A comparision of the *bhikkhuvibhanga* with the extant *bhikkhunivibhanga* shows rules which apply to one side of the order and not the other. Further, there are rules which show a marked correspondance where with some frequency monks incur a lesser penalty than nuns. We can see therefore that the nuns' discipline was extremely demanding. That the women of the *Therigatha* were able to practice and realize the Buddhist ideal within this strict and circumscribed context is a tribute to their dedication and sincerity.

Rules were an aspect of training. They had a very different origin from the Ten Commandments. The Ten Commandments were given by God to Moses. They were God's Law. The *Vinaya*, or rules of discipline, were rules of training, a human creation of Gautama and his followers for the purpose of facilitating living together in harmony and achieving the central goal of *nirvana*. The Buddhist rules didn't come about because Gautama sat down and thought them out, nor did a group of senior monks hold a meeting and make them up. Following more closely in our Western pattern of legal precedent, an individual rule came about as a response to an offense. The entire situation surrounding the offense, including the story, the rule, the exceptions to the rule, etc. was committed to memory and passed down. The best way to get a feel for such a mode of government is to see the structure of a single rule. Thus an example, Rule 63:

> At Savatthi in the Jeta Grove in Anathapindika's monastery:
> Now at that time, nuns ordained a novice who had not trained for two years in the six precepts. These were inexperienced nuns; they did not know what was allowed and what was not. Some modest nuns asked, "How can these nuns ordain a novice who has not trained for two years in the six precepts?"
> [Word traveled from the modest nuns to the monks to the Buddha and the Buddha rebuked the monks, and then addressed them, saying,] "I allow you monks to give a novice the

agreement to train for two years under the six precepts. It should be given as follows: the novice, having approached the Sangha, having arranged her upper robe over one shoulder, having bowed at the feet of the nuns, sat down, and saluted the nuns with palms together, should say, 'Nuns, I, so and so, a novice under the nun so and so, request the Sangha for the agreement to train for two years under the six precepts.' Her request should be spoken three times.

"The Sangha should be informed of the novice's desire by an experienced, competent nun. She should say, 'This novice, so and so, under the nun, so and so, requests of the Sangha the agreement to train under the six precepts. This is my motion: If it seems right to the nuns, let there be silence; if it does not seem right, let us speak.'

"The novice should then be told to say the following: 'For two years I undertake the training to refrain from killing, I undertake the training to refrain from taking what is not given, I undertake the training to refrain from unchastity, I undertake the training to refrain from lying, I undertake the training to refrain from alcohol or other drugs, I undertake the training to refrain from eating at the wrong time.'

"Therefore monks, let the nuns set forth this as a rule of their training: Whatever nun should ordain a novice who has not trained for two years under the six precepts, that is an offense of expiation.

"Whatever means:...nun is to be understood in this case.

"Two years means: two years.

"Has not trained means: either the training is not given or the training is given (but) is interrupted.

"Should ordain means:...(Rule 61, 2,1)...and an offense of wrongdoing for the group and for the woman teacher.

"There is no offense if she ordains a novice who has trained for two years under the six precepts, if she is mad, or if she is the first wrongdoer."[3]

---

[1] This is my adaptation of I.B. Horner, tr. *The Book of Discipline*. *(Cullavagga)* Vol. 5. (London: Luzac and Co., 1952), p. 356 and F.L. Woodward. *The Book of Gradual Sayings*. *(Anguttara-Nikaya)* Vol. IV. (London: Published for Pali Text Society by Oxford University Press, 1935), pp. 184-185

[2] My adaptation of Horner. *Op Cit.*, Vol. 10, 1-4.

[3] Horner. *Op. Cit.*, Vol. 3. *(Suttavibhanga, Bhikkhunivibhanga)*, pp. 364-366.

Glossary of Terms and Places

Abinna (Pali) — great magical powers; the six realms of sacred knowledge. These consist of five "mundane" powers, attainable through perfection in mental concentration, and one supramundane power, attained through insight (*vipassana*), i.e. attaining enlightenment. These powers are (1) magical powers, (2) the "Divine ear," the psychic ability to hear things near and far, (3) knowledge of the mind of others, (4) the "Divine Eye," insight into the future destiny of all beings, (5) remembrance of former lives, and (6) extinction of the *asavas*, the obsessions of the mind.

Acariya (Pali and Sanskrit) — women teachers.

Anatta (Pali), **anatman** (Sanskrit) — non-ego, no-self. This concept of *anatta*, the denial of a permanent, unchanging "self," is central and specific to Buddhism. All other Buddhist doctrines can be found in one form or another, in other philosophic systems and religions, but *anatta* is unique to Buddhism and the Buddha is sometimes known as the *"anatta-vadi,"* the teacher of impersonality.

Arahant (Pali), **arhat** (Sanskrit) — lit., a "worthy one," a "holy one." (1) One who is free from cravings and thus from rebirth, (2) one of the titles of the Buddha, and (3) the highest stage attained by a Theravadin Buddhist.

Ariya-sacca (Pali) — refers to the Four Noble Truths, perhaps the best known of all Buddhist teachings. The Four Noble Truths were reputed to have been taught in the Buddha's first sermon. The Truths are:

1) All existence is suffering.
2) The cause of suffering is craving and illusion.
3) Suffering can be eliminated.
4) The way to eliminate suffering is the Eightfold Way, which is the following:

1) Right understanding
2) Right mindfulness
3) Right speech
4) Right action
5) Right livelihood
6) Right effort
7) Right attention
8) Right concentration

Asavas (Pali), **asravas** (Sanskrit) — the obsessions of the mind. In Pali Buddhism, four sub-categories are distinguished: (1) the obsession with sensuality *(kamasava)*; (2) the obsession for life *(avijjasava)*; (3) the obsession with views, opinions; (4) ideologies *(ditthasava)*; and (5) the obsession of ignorance *(avijjasava)*. This is a key concept in Pali Buddhism generally, and in poems of the *Therigatha* specifically.

Balani (Pali) — powers.

Bhikkhu (Pali), **bhikkshu** (Sanskrit) — a male renunciant, an almsman. A religious mendicant who has left home and renounced all possessions in order to follow the way of the Buddha; a fully ordained monk.

Bhikkhuni (Pali), **bhikkshuni** (Sanskrit) — a female renunciant, an almswoman. A religious mendicant who has left home and renounced all possessions in order to follow the way of the Buddha; a Buddhist nun who has been fully ordained by both Sanghas.

Brahmana (Pali), **brahman** (Sanskrit) — a member of the priestly caste, the highest of the four major castes of India.

Brahmavadini (Pali) — a female renunciant under Brahmanism.

Buddha (Pali and Sanskrit) — an enlightened one; the historical person Siddhartha Gautama (Sanskrit) or Siddhattha Gotama (Pali).

Bujjhangatthangikam (Pali) — the seven factors (or qualities) of enlightenment which are (1) concentration, (2) energy, (3) rapture, (4) investigation, (5) tranquility, (6) equanimity, and (7) mindfulness.

Cakkavatti-raja (Pali) — lit., "wheel-turning king." In Indian mythology, this is the ideal ruler.

Dharma (Sanskrit), **dhamma** (Pali) — used in both Hinduism and Buddhism, meaning variously, according to context: the way; the law—religious, secular, or natural; phenomena; righteousness. The "Buddhadharma," the liberating law summed up by the Buddha, is the four Noble Truths.

Dhatu (Pali and Sanskrit) — the four elements; i.e. earth, water, fire, and wind.

Dibbacakkhum (Pali) — the six realms of sacred power.

Dukkha (Pali and Sanskrit) — suffering, pain, unsatisfactoriness, or ill-being.

Eightfold Way — see ariya-sacca

Four Noble Truths — see ariya-sacca

Gatha (Pali and Sanskrit) — song, poem, verse.

Indra (Sanskrit) — The deity in Hinduism who controls thunder, lightning, wind, and rain. He is the enemy of Mara. Adopted into Buddhism, Indra became one the protective deities.

Indriyani (Pali) — faculties. This term refers to the five senses as a whole rather than individually. A related term, *ayatana*, means both the organ and the object of sense.

Jatakas (Pali) — a collection of Indian folk stories about the Buddha's former lives.

Jatikhaya (Pali) — extinction of (renewed) birth.

Jatisamsaro (Pali) — wandering from birth to birth.

Jhana (Pali), **Dhyana** (Sanskrit), **Ch'an** (Chinese), **Zen** (Japanese) — absorption, meditation, contemplation on a single mental or physical object which leads to enlightenment.

Jina (Pali) — world conqueror, often said of the Buddha; "victor."

Karma (Sanskrit), **kamma** (Pali) — lit., "action"; causality; the law of cause and effect, sometimes interpreted personally as reward or punishment for deeds performed in this or a previous life.

Khattiya (Pali), **ksatriya** (Sanskrit) — the warrior caste, the second highest of the four major castes in India. Kings and other members of the ruling class, as well as warriors, were traditionally of this caste.

Magga (Pali), **marga** (Sanskrit) — path. There are four stages of the Buddhist path: (1) the path of stream-winning—free from the first three of the fetters (personality-belief, skeptical doubt, attachment to mere rule and ritual), (2) the path of once-returning—nearly free from the fourth and fifth fetters (craving, hatred), (3) the path of never-returning—completely free from the first five fetters, (4) the path of holiness or arahantship—free from the last five fetters (craving for material existence, craving for immaterial existence, conceit, restlessness, ignorance).

Mara (Pali and Sanskrit) — Death, the "Evil One," the Buddhist Devil or principle of destruction, so-called because he takes away the wisdom-life of all living beings. Sometimes the term *mara* is applied to the whole of worldly existence, or the realm of rebirth, as opposed to nirvana.

Maya (Pali and Sanskrit) — illusion, deceptive appearance in the sense of trick, magic. The association of *maya* with cosmic illusion, common to Hinduism, is absent from Pali Buddhism. The meaning in Pali is of the craft of the conjuror, the ability to make magic.

Mula (Pali) — three poisons or marks of existence — *lobha* (greed), *dosa* (hatred), *moha* (ignorance).

Muni (Pali and Sanskrit) — a sage, a saint.

Nirodha (Pali and Sanskrit) — extinction; a synonym of nirvana.

Nirvana (Sanskrit), **nibbana** (Pali) — lit., "extinction." (1) The state of enlightenment attained by the Buddha. (2) The highest and last stage of the path to enlightenment. (3) Extinction of all desire and attachment, and freedom from future rebirth.

Nivarana (Pali and Sanskrit) — The five hindrances, or obstacles—lust, malice, laziness, anxiety, and doubt.

Pabbajitta (Pali) — one who has left home to become a Buddhist renunciant.

Pali — lit., "holy text." This is the literary language in which the Buddhist Canon was preserved, first orally and later in written manuscripts.

Parinirvana (Sanskrit), **parinibbana** (Pali) — final extinction. Upon his death, the Buddha is said to have passed into parinirvana. However, the term is actually a synonym of *nirvana* and therefore does not refer merely to the extinction of the five groups of existence at the Buddha's death, as is commonly supposed, but to *nirvana* itself.

Rishi (Pali), **rishikas** (Sanskrit) — A sage or priest of special authority, particularly one of the "Seven Rishis" who are priests of the gods and are identified with the Stars of the Great Bear.

Samana (Pali), **sramana** (Sanskrit) — a renunciant, an ascetic. Often opposed to a *brahman*, a Brahmanic priest.

Samani (Pali), **sramani** (Sanskrit) — a female renunciant or ascetic.

Samsara (Pali and Sanskrit) — the endless cycle of birth and death; opposite of *nirvana*.

Samyojana (Pali and Sanskrit) — the ten fetters (see *Magga*).

Sangha (Pali and Sanskrit) — (1) the multitude, the assemblage, (2) the community of ordained Buddhist monks and nuns, i.e. the Buddhist order. This is sometimes divided into the monks' sangha *(bhikkhusangha)* and the nuns' sangha *(bhikkhunisangha)*. (3) More generally, it is the community of Buddhists.

Skandha (Sanskrit), **khandha** (Pali) — all physical and mental phenomena of existence which appear to the ignorant as one's ego or personality, the "elements of mind and body." (The five aggregates: *rupa*—body, *vedana*—feeling, *samjña*—perception, *samskara*—mental states, *vijñana*—consciousness.) (Aitken: perceptions and what they perceive, forms, sensation, thought, conceptual power, consciousness.) (Ross: The five aggregates which, in Buddhism, make up an individual.)

Sutta (Pali), **sutra** (Sanskrit) — a discourse by the Buddha or a disciple accepted as authoritative teaching; scripture.

Tathagatha (Pali) — lit., "The One who has 'Thus Come,' " an epithet of the Buddha.

Tevijja (Pali) — the three knowledges, of both Brahmanism and Buddhism. In Brahmanism, this is the higher knowledge of the brahmans, i.e. the three Vedas. This Brahmanic phrase was adopted by the Buddha and applied to the three attainments of Buddhism: (1) remembrance of former births, (2) insight into the future destiny of all beings; the Divine Eye, (3) the annihilation of the obsessions of the mind, which is synonymous with the destruction of any future rebirths.

Theri (Pali) — woman elder, woman who has grown old with knowledge.

Three Knowledges — see *tevijja*.

Vimokkha (Pali) — release, deliverance, emancipation.

Vinaya (Pali) — the rules of discipline of the sangha.

PLACE NAMES

Anga (Pali, Sanskrit) — one of the sixteen major kingdoms in India in Siddhartha Gautama's lifetime. It was contiguous to Magadha and became subject to Magadha about the sixth or fifth century B.C.E. Its capital was Campa.

Avanti (Pali, Sanskrit) — one of the sixteen major kingdoms in India in Siddhartha Gautama's lifetime.

Bodh Gaya (Pali, Sanskrit) — the place where the Buddha attained enlightenment; near present-day Gaya.

Jetavana (Pali, Sanskrit) — Jeta Grove Monastery, built by Buddhist patrons at Savatthi. Gautama was reputed to have spent nineteen rainy seasons here.

Kapilavatthu (Pali), **Kapilavastu** (Sanskrit) — the capital of the Sakya kingdom, where the Buddha grew up, near the border of India and Nepal, in the foothills of the Himalayas.

Kasi (Pali, Sanskrit) — one of the sixteen kingdoms. In pre-Buddhist times, Kasi was an independent kingdom. Later it was annexed to Magadha by Ajatasattu. The capital and chief city was Varanasi.

Koliya (Pali, Sanskrit) — the country of the Koliyan tribe, bordering on Kapilavatthu.

Kosala (Pali), **Kausala** (Sanskrit) — the most powerful of the sixteen kingdoms in the Buddha's lifetime. Pasenadi was the king. The Buddha spent much of the later part of his teaching career in Kausala.

Kosambi (Pali), **Kausambi** (Sanskrit) — the capital of the kingdom of Vansa. The modern city is Kosam.

Kusinara (Pali), **Kushinagara** (Sanskrit) — the capital of the kingdom of Malla; the village where the Buddha died.

Lumbini (Pali, Sanskrit) — the birthplace of Siddhartha Gautama in present-day Nepal.

Magadha (Pali, Sanskrit) — one of the sixteen major kingdoms of India during the lifetime of Siddhartha Gautama. Bimbisara was the king of Magadha. The modern state is Bihar. Located here were Jivaka's Mango Grove, Vulture Peak, and the Bamboo Forest Monastery (Venuvana).

Malla (Pali, Sanskrit) — one of the sixteen major kingdoms of India during the lifetime of Siddhartha Gautama.

Pataliputta (Pali), **Pataliputra** (Sanskrit) — present-day Patna in the state of Bihar.

Rajagaha (Pali), **Rajagriha** (Sanskrit) — the capital of the ancient kingdom of Magadha; the present-day city of Rajgir in the state of Bihar. Location of Vulture Peak. Rajagaha was reputed to have 36,000 merchants houses, half belonging to Buddhists, half to Jains. This city was at the height of its prosperity in the Buddha's time.

Sala Grove — the stand of twin sala trees near Kushinagara where Siddhartha Gautama died.

Savatthi (Pali), **Sravasti** (Sanskrit) — the capital of the kingdom of Kosala.

Ujjeni (Pali) — capital of Avanti.

Vansa (Pali), **Vatsa** (Sanskrit) — one of the sixteen major kingdoms of India during the lifetime of Siddhartha Gautama.

Venuvana (Pali) — the Bamboo Grove Monastery, built by King Bimbisara. Near Rajagaha, and near Gridhrakuta (Vulture Peak).

Vesali (Pali), **Vaisali** (Sanskrit) — the chief city of the Vajji; the present-day city of Basarh.

Index of Therigatha Poems

Bibliography

PRIMARY SOURCES IN ROMANIZED PALI

Bose, M.M., ed. *Paramatthadipani.* 2 Volumes. London: Published for the Pali Text Society by Oxford University Press, 1934-36.

Fausboll, V., ed. *Suttanipata.* 2 Volumes. London: Henry Frowde, 1885-1894.

Feer, Leon M., ed. *Samyutta Nikaya of the Sutta Pitaka, Bhikkhuni Samyutta.* Volume I, book V. London: Pali Text Society, 1973.

_____ . *Samyutta Nikaya of the Sutta Pitaka.* Part 1-2. London: Henry Frowde, 1884-1888.

Lilley, Mary E., ed. *Apadana of the Khuddakanikaya.* Part I-II. London: Published for the Pali Text Society by Oxford University Press, 1925-1927.

Muller, Edward, ed. *Paramatthadipani: Dhammapala's Commentary.* London: Henry Frowde, 1893.

Oldenberg, Hermann, and Richard Pischel, ed. *The Thera- and Therigatha.* London: Published for the Pali Text Society by Oxford University Press Warehouse, 1883.

_____ . *Theragatha.* London: Pali Text Society, 1966.

Rhys Davids, Caroline, ed. *The Visuddhi-Magga of Buddhaghosa.* 2 Volumes. London: Oxford University Press, 1920-1921.

Rhys Davids, T.W., and J. Estlin Carpenter, ed. *Digha-nikaya.* 3 Volumes. London: Published for the Pali Text Society by Henry Frowde, 1890-1911.

Pischel, Richard, ed. *The Therigatha.* London: Published for the Pali Text Society by Luzac and Co. Ltd., 1966.

Woodward, F.L., ed. *Paramatthadipani.* 2 Volumes. London: Oxford University Press, 1940.

PRIMARY SOURCES IN ENGLISH TRANSLATION

Allen, George, ed. and tr. *Buddha's Words of Wisdom*. London: George Allen and Unwin Ltd., 1959.

Avalon, Arthur and Ellen Avalon (Lady Ellen and Sir John Woodruffe). *Hymns to the Goddess Madras*. London: Ganesh and Co., 1964.

Burlingame, E.W., tr. *Buddhaghosa's Dhammapada Commentary (Dhammapadatthakatha)*. 3 Volumes. Harvard Oriental Series. Volume 2. Cambridge: Harvard University Press, 1921.

Chalmers, Lord, tr. *Further Dialogues of the Buddha (Majjhima Nikaya)*. 2 Volumes. London: Oxford University Press, 1926-1927.

_____ . *Buddha's Teachings (Being the Sutta-Nipata or Discourse Collection)*. Cambridge: Harvard University Press, 1932.

Chattopadhyaya, Debiprasad, ed. *Taranatha's History of Buddhism in India*. Lama Chimpa and Alaka Chattopadhyaya, tr. Atlantic City, New Jersey: Humanities Press, 1981.

Childers, Robert Ceasar. *A Dictionary of the Pali Language*. 1909. Reprint. London: Kegan, Paul Trench, and Trubner and Co., Ltd., 1974.

Conze, Edward. *Buddhist Texts Through the Ages*. Boston: Shambhala, 1990.

Feer, M. Leon, ed. *Samyutta Nikaya of the Sutta Pitaka, Bhikkhuni Samyutta*. Book V. London: Pali Text Society, 1973.

Francis, H.T. and E.J. Thomas, tr. *Jataka Tales*. Cambridge: Cambridge University Press, 1916.

Horner, I.B., tr. *The Book of Discipline (Vinayapitaka)*. 6 Volumes. London: Oxford University Press Warehouse, 1938-1966. Contents: Volumes 1-3 *Vinaya, Suttavibhanga* (1938, 1940, 1942), 4—*Mahavagga* (1951), 5—*Cullavagga* (1952), 6—*Parivara* (1966). Volumes 4-6 have imprint London: Luzac and Co.

_____ . *Ten Jataka Stories*. London: Luzac and Co., 1957.

_____ . *Book of the Discipline. (Vinaya-Pitaka)*. Part 5, Sacred Books of the Buddhists. London: Pali Text Society, 1975.

Ireland, John D., ed. *Samyutta Nikaya: An Anthology*. Kandy, Sri Lanka: Buddhist Publication Society, 1967.

Malalasekera, George P. *Dictionary of Pali Proper Names*. London: Luzac and Co. Ltd., 1960.

Morris, Richard, ed. *Buddhavamsa Commentary*. London: Published for the Pali Text Society by Henry Frowde, 1882.

_____ , ed. *The Book of Gradual Sayings (Anguttara Nikaya)*. Vol. IV. London: Published for the Pali Text Society by Henry Frowde, 1885-1910.

Muller, Max, ed. *Vinaya Texts*. T.W. Rhys Davids and Hermann Oldenberg, tr. Part I—*The Mahavagga i-iv*; part II—*The Mahavagga v-x, Kullavagga i-iii*; part III - *The Kullavagga iv-xii*. *The Sacred Books of the East*, Vol.XIII, XVII, XX. Oxford: Clarendon Press, 1881-1885. Reprinted by Delhi: Motilal Banarsidass, 1969.

Norman, K.R., tr. *The Elders' Verses I Theragatha*. London: Published for the Pali Text Society by Luzac and Co. Ltd., 1969.

_____ , tr. *The Elders' Verses II Therigatha*. London: Published for Pali Text Society by Luzac and Co. Ltd., 1966.

Nyanatiloka. *Buddhist Dictionary*. Sri Lanka: Frewin and Co. Ltd., 1951.

Parrinder, Geoffrey. *The Wisdom of the Early Buddhists*. New York: New Directions, 1977.

Pischel, Richard, ed. *The Therigatha*. London: Published for the Pali Text Society by Luzac and Co. Ltd., 1966.

Rhys Davids, Caroline, tr. *A Buddhist Manual of Psychological Ethics*. London: Pali Text Society, 1900.

_____ . *Psalms of the Sisters*. London: Published for the Pali Text Society by Henry Frowde, Oxford University Press Warehouse, 1909.

_____ . *Psalms of the Brethren*. London: Published for the Pali Text Society by Oxford University Press Warehouse, 1913.

_____ . *Buddhist Psychology: An Inquiry into the Analysis and Theory of Mind in Pali Literature*. New York: Macmillan, 1914.

_____ . *The Book of Kindred Sayings. (Samyutta-Nikaya)*. 5 Volumes. London: Published for the Pali Text Society by Oxford University Press, 1917-1930.

_____ , ed. *The Visuddhi-Magga of Buddhaghosa*. 2 Volumes. London: Oxford University Press, 1920.

_____ . *Minor Anthologies of the Pali Canon (Khuddaka Nikaya)* Parts 1-4: 1. *Dhammapada and Khuddaka-Patha* 2. *Udana and Itivuttaka* 3. *Buddhavamsa and Carita Pitaka*. Bimala Churn Law, tr., Part 3. London: Oxford University Press, 1931-1938.

_____ . *Wayfarer's Words*. 3 Volumes. London: Oxford University Press, 1940.

_____ . *Stories of the Buddha, Being Selections from the Jataka*. New York: Dover, 1989.

Rhys Davids, T.W., and Caroline Rhys Davids, tr. *Mahasattipatthana Suttana*. London: Luzac and Co., 1951.

_____ . and William Stede, ed. *Pali Text Society's Pali-English Dictionary*. London: Pali Text Society, 1972.

Woodward, F.L. *The Book of Gradual Sayings. (Anguttara-Nikaya)*. Vol I-V. Published for the Pali Text Society by Oxford University Press, 1932-1936.

SECONDARY SOURCES

Aitken, Robert. *A Zen Wave*. New York: Weatherhill, 1978.

_____ . *Taking the Path of Zen*. San Francisco: North Point Press, 1982.

_____ . *The Mind of Clover*. San Francisco: North Point Press, 1984.

Allione, Tsultrim. *Women of Wisdom*. New York: Arkana, 1986.

Altekar, A.S. *The Position of Women in Hindu Civilization*. Delhi: Motilal Banarsidass, 1938.

de Bary, Theodore, ed. *The Buddhist Tradition*. New York: Random House, 1972.

Bernal, Martin. *Black Athena—The Afro-Asiatic Roots of Classical Civilization*. Volume 1. New Jersey: Rutgers University Press, 1987.

Beyer, Stephen. *The Cult of Tara: Magic and Ritual in Tibet*. Berkeley: University of California Press, 1973.

Bhattacharyya, N.N. *The Indian Mother Goddess*. Columbia, Missouri: South Asian Books, 1977.

_____ . *History of Researches on Indian Buddhism*. New Delhi: Munshiram Manoharlal, 1981.

Boucher, Sandy. *Turning the Wheel*. San Francisco: Harper and Row, 1988.

Campbell, Joseph. *The Masks of God: Oriental Mythology*. New York: Viking Press, 1962.

Chang, Pao. Li Jung-hsi, tr. *Biographies of Buddhist Nuns*. Osaka: Tohokai, 1981.

Chattopadhyaya, Debiprasad. *Lokayata: A Study of Ancient Indian Materialism*. New Delhi: People's Publishing House, 1959.

Conze, Edward. *Buddhist Meditation*. London: George Allen and Unwin Ltd., 1956.

_____ . *A Short History of Buddhism*. Bombay: Chetana, 1960.

Deo, Shantatam Chalchandra. *History of Jaina Monachism*. Poona: Deccan College, 1956.

Dhadphale, G.M. *Some Aspects of (Buddhist) Literary Criticism*. Bombay: Adreesh Prakashan, 1975.

Durdin-Robertson, Lawrence. *The Goddesses of India, Tibet, China and Japan*. Clonegal, Ireland: Cesara Publications, 1976.

Dutt, Nalinaksha. *Early Monastic Buddhism*. Calcutta: Firma K.L. Mukhopadhyay, 1971.

Dutt, Sukumar. *Buddhist Monks and Monasteries in India*. London: George Allen and Unwin Ltd., 1962.

_____ . *Early Buddhist Monachism 600 B.C.—100 B.C.* New Delhi: Munshiram Manoharial, 1984.

Eisler, Riane. *The Chalice and the Blade*. San Francisco: Harper and Row, 1987.

Eliade, Mircea. *Patterns in Comparative Religion*. Translation of *Traite d'Histoire des Religions* from the French by Rosemary Sheed. London and New York: Sheed and Ward, 1958.

Falk, Nancy A. and Rita Bross, ed. *Unspoken Worlds*. San Francisco: Harper and Row, 1982.

Fields, Rick. *How the Swans Came to the Lake*. Boulder: Shambhala, 1981.

Friedman, Lenore. *Meetings with Remarkable Women: Buddhist Teachers in America*. Boston: Shambhala, 1987.

Galland, China. *Longing for Darkness: Tara and the Black Madonna*. New York: Viking, 1990.

Geiger, Wilhelm. *Pali Literature and Language*.Batakrishna Ghosh, tr. Delhi: Oriental Books Reprint Corporation, 1968.

Gimbutas, Marija. *The Goddesses and Gods of Old Europe—Myths and Cult Images*. Berkeley: University of California Press, 1982.

_____ . *The Language of the Goddess*. San Francisco: Harper and Row, 1989.

Goldstein, Joseph. *The Experience of Insight*. Boston: Shambhala, 1983.

Gupta, Kaushalya. *Women in Buddhist Literature*. Tubingen, Germany, 1960.

Gupta, Sri Sankar Sen. *Tree Symbol Worship in India*. Calcutta: Indian Publications, 1965.

_____ . *Woman in Indian Folklore*. Calcutta: Indian Publications, 1969.

Hardy, R.S. *Eastern Monachism*. London: Partridge and Oakey, 1850.

Hecker, Hellmuth. *Buddhist Women at the Time of the Buddha*. Sri Lanka: Buddhist Publication Society, 1982.

Hirakawa, Akira. *Monastic Discipline for the Buddhist Nuns: An English Translation of the Chinese Text of the Mahasamghika-Bhiksuni-Vinaya*. Patna: Jayaswal Research Institute, 1982.

Hopkinson, Deborah, Michele Hill, and Eileen Kiera. *Not Mixing Up Buddhism*. New York: White Pine Press, 1986.

Horner, I.B. *Women Under Primitive Buddhism*. London: George Routledge and Sons, Ltd., 1930. Reprinted by Asia Books Corp., 1975.

_____ . *Early Buddhist Poetry*. Sri Lanka: Ananda Semage, 1963.

Ikeda, Daisaku. *The Living Buddha*. New York: John Weatherhill Inc., 1973.

Indra, Prof. *Status of Women in Ancient India*. Banaras: Motilal Banarsidass, 1955.

The Jerusalem Bible. New York: Doubleday and Co., 1966.

Kabilsingh, Chatsumarn. *A Comparative Study of Bhikkhuni Patimokkha*. Varanasi: Chaukhambha Orientalia, 1984.

Khantipalo, Phra. *Banner of the Arhants: Buddhist Monks and Nuns from the Buddha's Time till Now*. Sri Lanka: Buddhist Publication Society, 1979.

Kosambi, D.D. *Ancient India*. New York: World Publishing Co., 1969.

Law, Bimala. *Women in Buddhist Literature*. Calcutta: Bastian and Co., 1927.

Ling, T. O. *Buddhism and the Mythology of Evil*. London: George Allen and Unwin Ltd., 1962.

Macy, Joanna. *World As Lover, World As Self*. Berkeley: Parallax Press, 1991.

Madhavananda, S., and R. Mayumdar, ed. *Great Women of India*. Almora Himalayas: Advaita Ashrama, 1953.

Mallory, J.P. *In Search of the Indo-Europeans: Language, Archeology and Myth*. London: Thames and Hudson Ltd., 1989.

Marshall, J. *Mohenjodara and Indus Civilization*. Volume I. London: Probstain, 1931.

Martin, Rafe. *The Hungry Tigress: Buddhist Legends and Jataka Tales*. Berkeley: Parallax Press, 1990.

Meltzer, David, ed. *Birth: An Anthology of Ancient Texts, Songs, Prayers and Stories*. San Francisco: North Point Press, 1980.

Mizuno, Kogen. *The Beginnings of Buddhism*. Richard Gage, tr. Tokyo: Kosei Publishing Co., 1980.

_____ . *Buddhist Sutras*. Tokyo: Kosei Publishing Co., 1982.

Narain, A.K., ed. *Studies in History of Buddhism*. [Papers presented at the International Conference on the History of Buddhism at the University of Wisconsin, 1976] Delhi: B.R. Publishing Co., 1980.

Nhat Hanh, Thich. *Old Path White Clouds: Walking in the Footsteps of the Buddha*. Berkeley: Parallax Press, 1990.

Nyanaponika, Thera. *The Heart of Buddhist Meditation*. New York: Samuel Weiser, Inc., 1962.

O'Flaherty, Wendy, ed. *The Critical Study of Sacred Texts*. Berkeley: Graduate Theological Union, 1979.

_____ . *The Rig Veda*. Middlesex, England: Penguin Books, 1981.

Paul, Diana. *Women in Buddhism: Images of the Feminine in Mahayana Tradition*. Berkeley: University of California Press, 1985.

Peiris, William. *The Western Contribution to Buddhism*. Delhi: Motilal Banarsidass, 1973.

Piyadassi, Thera. *The Virgin's Eye*. Sri Lanka: Buddhist Publication Society, 1980.

Rabten, Geshe. *The Preliminary Practices of Tibetan Meditation*. Dharamsala: Library of Tibetan Works and Archives, 1982.

Ross, Nancy Wilson. *Three Ways of Asian Wisdom: Hinduism, Buddhism and Zen and their Significance for the West*. New York: Simon and Schuster, 1966.

_____ . *Buddhism: A Way of Life and Thought*. New York: Alfred Knopf, 1981.

Rhys Davids, Caroline. *A Manual of Buddhism for Advanced Students*. New York: Macmillan, 1932.

_____ . *Buddhism: Its Birth and Dispersal*. London: T. Butterworth, 1934.

_____ . *To Become or Not to Become*. London: Luzac and Co., 1937.

_____ . *What Was the Original Gospel in Buddhism?* London: The Epworth Press, 1938.

_____ . *The Birth of India Psychology and Its Development in Buddhism*. New Delhi: Oriental Books Reprint Corp., 1978.

Rhys Davids, T.W. *History and Literature of Buddhism*. Calcutta: Susil Gupta Ltd., 1896.

Rhys Davids, T.W., and Hermann Oldenberg, tr. *Vinaya Texts*. Part I. *Sacred Books of the East*, Volume xiii. London: Published for the Pali Text Society by Henry Frowde, Oxford University Press Warehouse, 1881.

Shastri, Shakuntala Rao. *Women in the Vedic Age*. Bombay: Baratiya Vidya Bhavan, 1969.

Shekhar, I. *Sanskrit Drama: Its Origin and Decline*. New Delhi: Munshiram Mancharial Publishers Ltd., 1977.

Sidor, Ellen. *A Gathering of Spirit: Women Teaching in American Buddhism*. Cumberland, Rhode Island: Primary Point Press, 1987.

Sircar, D.C. *Laksmi and Sarasvati in Art and Literature*. Calcutta: University of Calcutta, 1970.

Sjoo, Monica and Barbara Mor. *The Great Cosmic Mother—Rediscovering the Religion of the Earth*. San Francisco: Harper and Row, 1987.

Talim, Meena. *Women in Early Buddhist Literature*. Bombay: University of Bombay, 1972.

Thomas, E.J. *The Life of Buddha as Legend and History*. London: Kegan Paul, 1927.

Thomas, P. *Indian Women through the Ages*. Bombay: P.S. Jayasinghe Asia Publishing House, 1964.

Wardner, A.K. *Pali Metre*. London: Published for the Pali Text Society by Luzac and Co. Ltd., 1967.

Wekar, Hari Ramchandra. *Women in Ancient India*. Kasturba Indore, India: Kasturba Ghandi: National Memorial Trust, 1962.

Welbon, Guy. *The Buddhist Nirvana and Its Western Interpreters*. Chicago: University of Chicago Press, 1968.

Winternitz, Maurice. *History of Indian Literature*. New Delhi: Oriental Book Reprint Corp., 1977.

Young, Katherine. *Images of the Feminine in Buddhist, Hindu and Islamic Traditions*. New York: New Horizon's Press, 1974.

Zimmer, Heinrich. Joeseph Campbell, ed. *Myths and Symbols in Indian Art*. Princeton: Princeton University Press, 1972.

Articles, Lectures, and Unpublished Theses

Bode, Mabel Hayes. "The Women Leaders of the Buddhist Reformation." London: Ninth International Congress of Orientalists, 1892.

Bloomfield, Maurice. "False Ascetics and Nuns in Hindu Fiction." *JAOS*. 44: 202-42.

Darian, Jean. "Social and Economic Factors in the Rise of Buddhism." *Sociological Analysis*. 1977. 38, 3: 226-238.

Dewaraja, L.S. "The Position of Women in Buddhism." Sri Lanka: Buddhist Publication Society, 1981. (The Wheel Publication #280).

Dimmitt, Dr. Cornelia. "Sanghamitta Day." A Lecture at the Washington D.C. Buddhist Vihara, 1972.

_____. "Thoughts on the Therigatha." A Lecture at the Washington D.C. Buddhist Vihara, 1980.

Downing, Christine. "Goddess Sent Madness." *Psychological Perspectives*, Fall 1981.

Falk, Nancy Auer. "An Image of Women in Old Buddhist Literature: The Daughters of Mara." *Women and Religion*. Judith Plaskow and Joan Arnold, ed., pp. 105-112. Missoula, Montana: Scholars Press, 1974.

_____. "The Case of the Vanishing Nuns: The Fruits of Ambivalence in Ancient Indian Buddhism," *Unspoken Worlds*. Nancy Falk and Rita Gross, ed. San Francisco: Harper and Row, 1980.

Foster, Nelson. "The Octets of the *Atthakavagga*." Mimeographed. University of Hawaii, November 20, 1979.

Gimbutas, Marija. "The First Wave of Eurasion Steppe Pastoralists into Copper Age Europe." *The Journal of Indo-European Studies* 5. Winter, 1977.

Gross, Rita. "Buddhism and Feminism." *Kahawai*. Vol. 2, No. 4. Honolulu, HI.

Havens, Teresina Rowell. "Gotama's Early Psychological Experimentation." *The Eastern Buddhist*. Volume 1, No. 2. November 1966.

Horner, I.B. "Women in Early Buddhism." *The Middle Way*. May and August, 1957.

Kornfield, Jack. "The Seven Factors of Enlightenment." *Ten Directions*. October 1981, pp. 3-4.

Law, Bimala Churn. "Buddhist Women." *Indian Antiquary* 58. March-May 1928, pp. 49-54, 65-68, 86-89.

Mantri, Naresh. "On Women Attaining Buddhahood." *Young East*. Volume 2. Winter 1976.

Marsh, Katherine. "The *Theriigatha* and *Theraagatha*." Mimeographed thesis. Cornell University, 1980.

Miller, Barbara Stoler. "Ballads of Early Nuns." *Zero*. Vol V, 1980.

Milliken, Roger. Unpublished Manuscript. 1979.

Oldenberg, H. "The Prose and Verse Type Narrative and the Jatakas." *Journal of the Pali Text Society*. 1912.

Sharma, Arvind. "How and Why Did Women in Ancient India Become Buddhist Nuns?" *Sociological Analysis*. 1977 38; 3: 239-251.

Wright, Dudley. "Buddhism and Women." *The Buddhist Review*. 3 (3) 243-50.